ALL MY ~~IDIOT~~ 1500 QUESTIONS

DAVID BOWIE

ALL MY ~~IDIOT~~ 1500 QUESTIONS

pete thompson

Front Cover: David at the Wembley Arena in London
Serious Moonlight Tour, 2nd June 1983
Printed with kind permission © Pete Still

Copyright © 2022 Pete Thompson

All rights reserved. No part of this book may be reproduced or used in any manner without written permission of the copyright owner except for the use of quotations in a book review.

ISBN: 979-8-7241-9446-4

This paperback edition was first published in 2022

Mum and Dad
your love of music set me on the path

Carole
for sharing me with Bowie
you're such a wonderful person

Sean & Kerry / Clair & Kris
they're just older children

Cassie, Barney, Lincoln and Bobby
the young dudes
" Grandad, can I go in The David Bowie Room? "

CONTENTS

ABOUT THE AUTHOR ix
ACKNOWLEDGEMENTS xiii
PREFACE xvii
INTRODUCTION xxi
BEFORE STARTING xxv
pre 1960s (64 Questions) 2
pre 1960s (Answers) 11
the 1960s (168 Questions) 14
the 1960s (Answers) 33
the 1970s (373 Questions) 40
the 1970s (Answers) 79
the 1980s (233 Questions) 94
the 1980s (Answers) 117
the 1990s (262 Questions) 126
the 1990s (Answers) 155
the 2000s (200 Questions) 166
the 2000s (Answers) 189
the 2010s (200 Questions) 196
the 2010s (Answers) 223
AND FINALLY 231

ABOUT THE AUTHOR

I was only four years old when my family moved house and set up home on the Greatfield Estate in Hull. Little did I know then that I was living just a short five minute walk from Mick Ronson's family home, but it was a fact that I was to become very much aware of as I grew older. Mick Ronson was twelve years older than me, I never did meet him, but it was kind of cool having a famous guitar player living just around the corner. That's basically how I got into David Bowie and his music, and it's been an obsession ever since.

I can remember back then, there always seemed to be rumours flying around about Bowie and Ronson coming back to Hull to visit Mick's mum and stories of impromptu little jamming sessions taking place in the front garden. I never saw anything, and I spent many an hour round that way playing football in the streets, just in case they ever showed! Looking back now, I'm pretty sure it was just a case of the older contingent spreading rumours and lies ...., and having a little bit of fun at our expense.

As youngsters at school, we couldn't all afford to buy the latest Bowie LP so we took it in turns. One of us would buy it and the others would congregate at that person's house, for what was always a magical experience. We'd all admire the LP cover artwork and read the sleeve notes. The owner would remove the vinyl from its sleeve (there was always a smell about a new vinyl record), place it carefully on the turntable and drop the needle before re-joining the others, who by then had gathered around the lyric sheet – it was show time. This was our ritual, and it never failed to impress.

Different albums mean different things to me and each one reminds me to some extent of what was going on in my life at the time of its release. I even use them as tools for remembering important dates – I met my wife in the year **Young Americans**, we were engaged by **"Heroes"** and married in **Lodger.** My son was born in **Let's Dance** and my daughter in **Never Let Me Down** – my nieces and nephews were born in **Tonight, Never Let Me Down, 1. Outside** and **Earthling** respectively ...... but enough of that!

I find it hard to choose a favourite album, because I genuinely love them all. That said, if I were forced to choose one, I think I'd go with **Hunky Dory** (well I would today anyway – it would have been **Diamond Dogs** yesterday and maybe **Heathen** tomorrow). Every track on **Hunky Dory** is quite wonderful and as the end of the album approaches, just when we think it can't get any better, we're treated to *The Bewlay Brothers* – it's such a special album ! I met Ken Scott once and he told me one or two nice stories about **Hunky Dory.** My favourite era is a little more straight forward – the early Ziggy Stardust period only lasted 18 months or so but living my formative years in Hull, the home of the Spiders, this was a special time for me growing up.

    I am a collector of all things Bowie and I continue to buy all the music, the videos, the books, magazines, postage stamps, royal mint coins, T-shirts, if they're Bowie related items, I try to buy them (funds permitting of course), and I love them all. I somewhat reluctantly buy the re-releases, and the remastered re-releases of the re-releases (you know what I mean) simply because they all have a different catalogue number (sad I know). I store my entire collection, all together in wall to wall cube shelving, in what my grandkids call 'The David Bowie Room'.

    Over the years, I've done all the Bowie haunts, the schools, the family homes, got the photos (some of which appear in the book), and I've attended many events from gigs to conventions, and from book signings to the annual Beckenham Free Festival. I feel privileged to have met and spoken, if only briefly, to many Bowie associated people, including Mick 'Woody' Woodmansey, Trevor Bolder, Tony Visconti, Ken Scott, Mary Finnigan, Maggi & Lisa Ronson, John 'Hutch' Hutchinson, Earl Slick, Mike Garson, John Cambridge and even Stuey

George. Mary Finnigan was good enough to take me down Foxgrove Road to show me where she and David used to live in the late 1960s – all demolished now of course but great to go there and get the photos. I thank them all for taking the time to autograph the various items that I shoved under their noses! It goes without saying, my David Bowie collection means everything to me!

Figure 1: The David Bowie Room

ACKNOWLEDGEMENTS

The following books are from my own personal collection. I've enjoyed reading them over many years and it's impossible to know what specific info or trivia I might have gleaned from which book. Suffice to say they have all complimented each other, they have all been part of the bigger picture and each one has in some way helped shape the trivia within the book. They have been invaluable and accordingly, I list and acknowledge them here.

A Chronology – Kevin Cann
A Portrait of Bowie – Brian Hiatt
Abbey Road To Ziggy Stardust – Ken Scott and Bobby Owsinski
Alias David Bowie – Peter & Leni Gillman
An Illustrated Record – Roy Carr and Charles Shaar Murray
Any Day Now, The London Years – Kevin Cann
At The Birth of Bowie – Phil Lancaster
Backstreet Passes – Angela Bowie
Bowie & Hutch – John 'Hutch' Hutchinson
Bowie In Berlin – Thomas Jerome Seabrook

ALL MY ~~IDIOT~~ 1500 QUESTIONS

Bowie In His Own Words – Barry Miles
Bowie Style – Mark Paytress
Bowie, Bolan and the Brooklyn Boy – Tony Visconti
Bowie, Cambo & All The Hype – John Cambridge
Bowie's Piano Man – Mike Garson
Changes, A Life In Pictures – Chris Welch
David Bowie – Jeff Hudson
David Bowie A Life – Dylan Jones
David Bowie A Rock N Roll Odyssey – Kate Lynch
David Bowie Black Book – Barry Miles
David Bowie FAQ – Ian Chapman
David Bowie Is – Victoria Broakes and Geoffrey Marsh
David Bowie The Archive – Chris Charlesworth
Duffy, Bowie – Kevin Cann & Chris Duffy
Glass Idol – David Currie
Hero: David Bowie – Lesley-Ann Jones
In Other Words – Kerry Juby
Lick Me – Cherry Vanilla
Life On Tour With Bowie – Sean Mayes
Living On The Brink – George Tremlett
Loving The Alien – Christopher Sandford
Moonage Daydream – Dave Thompson
Moonage Daydream – Mick Rock & David Bowie
My Life with Bowie, Spider From Mars – 'Woody' Woodmansey
Psychedelic Suburbia – Mary Finnigan
Ricochet: An Intimate Portrait – Denis O'Regan
Stardust - Tony Zanetta and Henry Edwards
Starman – Paul Trynka
Strange Fascination – David Buckley
The Age Of Bowie – Paul Morley
The Anabas Look Book Series – Jim Palmer
The Complete David Bowie – Nicholas Pegg
The David Bowie Story – George Tremlett
The Man Who Sold The World – Peter Doggett

ACKNOWLEDGEMENTS

The Pitt Report – Kenneth Pitt
The Starzone Interviews – David Currie
The Story of Rock's Enduring Enigma – Mike Evans
We Could Be…Bowie and his Heroes – Tom Hagler
When Ziggy Played Guitar – Dylan Jones
When Ziggy Played The Marquee – Terry O'Neill
Your Pretty Face Is Going To Hell – Dave Thompson

Magazines such as Mojo, NME, Q, Record Collector, Uncut and the many special editions and collector's editions they've published over the years, have also been used as a source of information and cross referencing.

The following websites are more than worthy of a mention, and an acknowledgement. At various junctures of the project, I was able to cross reference details by visiting sites built and maintained by dedicated, knowledgeable and enthusiastic fans. I thank them all.

- *5years.com*
- *bowiebible.com*
- *bowiegoldenyears.com*
- *bowiewonderworld.com*
- *davidbowie.com*
- *davidbowie.se/bassman*
- *davidbowienews.com*
- *davidbowieworld.nl*
- *illustrated-db-discography.nl*

Many thanks to photographer Pete Still who kindly granted permission for me to use the stunning 'Serious Moonlight' shot for the book cover, totally free of charge. Pete has so many great photos to choose from, I changed my mind several times but I just kept coming back to that hat and that sax! Check him out at https://www.facebook.com/PeteStillPhotography/, as well as on Getty Images and on Ebay.

Thank you also to Carole, my wife and my best friend for forty seven years. She was not directly involved in the project but while I worked on the book, she spent many an hour alone in the living room with only the TV and her Agatha Christie Word Search book for company. Her support and understanding, however, never waivered. She was happy to supply the *breakfast and coffee-ee-ee* and she continually offered the encouragement I needed to see the project through. *Tell my wife I love her very much, she knows !*

Last, but certainly not least, thank you to David Bowie, for everything. .

PREFACE

On 16th August 1969, David Bowie and friends organised the Growth Summer Free Festival in the Croydon Road Recreation Ground, a public park in Beckenham. The focal point was a bandstand from where Bowie and other artists would perform. The festival was a success and in her book 'Psychedelic Suburbia', Mary Finnigan suggests that the lyrics of Bowie's song *Memory Of A Free Festival,* succinctly reflect the atmosphere of that afternoon.

The bandstand itself was erected in 1905 and is believed to be the only 'McCallum and Hope Iron Foundry' designed bandstand, still existing in the UK today. It now enjoys iconic status, it is affectionately known as the 'Bowie Bandstand' and in 2019, on the advice of Historic England, the structure received a Grade II listing.

More than fifty years on, it's fair to say that the bandstand has fallen into disrepair somewhat and attempts to raise funds for its restoration are ongoing. Wendy Faulkner resurrected the Free Festival a few years ago and my wife and I travel down to Beckenham every year for the event. There are food and drink stalls, arts and crafts, auctions and raffles, and artists perform Bowie songs as well as original compositions, all from the bandstand. A little bit of that British summer sunshine and it's a thoroughly enjoyable afternoon.

Bowie has always meant so much to me and I've had such pleasure over the years attending the many Bowie related events, organised with great enthusiasm and dedication by other fans. I've tried to think of ways in which I could do something, somewhere, and perhaps in doing so, raise funds to be shared between the Bowie Bandstand Restoration Appeal (we all love the bandstand) and Macmillan Cancer Support, a charity close to many people's hearts.

Prior to the 2021 festival, I had been mulling over a few ideas, one of which was the notion of producing some kind of book, perhaps going down the self-publishing route. I wasn't, however, about to start writing my own in-depth analysis or critique about David Bowie. For one thing, it's been done hundreds of times already, but for another, I possess neither the academic nor the literacy skills necessary to embark on such a challenge. After all, I'm not an author or journalist, I'm just a huge David Bowie fan from Hull. But I did have an idea to maybe revisit something which I'd actually started back in the 1970s, something which might now be worth exploring further.

PREFACE

Initially, I guess I was quite excited at the prospect of doing something aimed at trying to raise funds, but I had doubts. My hesitancy perhaps came from my inexperience and even my lack of self-belief to bring such a project to fruition. I continued to mull over a few ideas during the autumn of 2021, but it didn't really go anywhere. Then, just before Christmas, I was re-watching some of my older clips of Bowie and I came across the 'Inspirations' documentary from 1997, directed by Michael Apted. In it, David said:-

"The other thing I would say is that if you feel safe in the area that you're working in, you're not working in the right area. Always go a little further into the water than you feel you're capable of being in. Go a little bit out of your depth and when you don't feel that your feet are quite touching the bottom, you're just about in the right place to do something exciting"

OK, I'm not an artist working in any particular area, so he's not talking directly to me, but that said, perhaps the sentiment of his advice is something I could draw upon. I'd never considered writing or self-publishing a book before, ever, so I was definitely not working in a safe area and I was certainly feeling a bit overwhelmed and out of my depth at the very thought. David's words somehow meant everything and ultimately they provided the advice and the encouragement that I needed to start prepping. The green light to take the project forward was turned on right there, and David Bowie had helped me again.

Ultimately, if the project fails then it fails, and no harm done. If on the other hand it succeeds in raising funds, however small, then it will have all been worthwhile. Either way, I can be pleased that I eventually took the plunge, I've given it my best shot and I've seen the project through to completion.

INTRODUCTION

The Glam Rock years of the early 1970s were outrageously exhilarating, well I thought so anyway. These were my formative years and from Slade to Suzi Quatro and from The Sweet to T. Rex, I grew up listening to and watching it all, and I loved it. But one artist stood head and shoulders above the rest – enter my life, David Bowie.

As for so many other fans, those *Starman* performances on 'Lift Off with Ayshea' and 'Top of the Pops', within a week of each other in 1972, were pivotal. For me, it was initially all about the music. The back catalogue was on my radar and I would buy what I could with the pocket money I had. But it wasn't long before I needed to know more about the man himself. Remember there was no internet in those days, so it was simply a case of listening to the radio, watching the TV and reading the newspapers and magazines. I learned that there was life before *Space Oddity*, and even life before

Deram, and I soaked it all up. Then David Bowie books started to appear in the bookshops and for the next few years, I was in my element, my life was all mapped out. Records were on my turntable daily and books/magazines were queuing up to be read. It was all consuming and I couldn't get enough of David Bowie.

I easily knew more about Bowie than my friends at school, and that was important. I knew about Hermione and Lindsay Kemp; I knew about the 1960s Pye singles and I knew about The Velvets and Warhol. I knew about his family, about early band members and I knew about David's influences. But I also seemed to have a never ending list of names in my head, whom I'd definitely read about, but truth be told I wasn't entirely sure who they were or how they fitted into the David Bowie story. I soon realised that although my mind was awash with random snippets of information, it didn't really mean too much because I was missing a timeline. I didn't know whether Hermione came before Kemp, whether either of them came before the Pye singles, and when did David actually meet or become aware of the Velvets and Warhol ? I had no idea.

So for the rest of the decade and into the early 1980s, I set about re-reading, making my own notes and re-learning. The aim was to end up with a set of David Bowie trivia facts, organised into some kind of chronological order, something that would enable me to see the fuller picture. To an extent, I did achieve my goal and I learned a lot. The project was only ever about self-satisfaction but any thoughts I may have had of doing

INTRODUCTION

anything more with it were put on the back burner somewhat when my family came along. My son was born in 1983 and my daughter in 1987, and day to day life, specifically family life, simply took over, and I wouldn't have changed that for the world, not even for David Bowie! More than 30 years on, my children are now grown up with young dudes of their own and that in turn has given me the opportunity to finish what I started. So my notes have resurfaced, they've been overhauled, updated and the result is this light-hearted book of trivia questions, for fun and for charity.

There is no attempt to analyse or critique here, the remit has simply been to present in chronological order, decade by decade, in such a way as to encourage the reader to further research for themselves, any particular era or point of interest. It should be noted that I don't claim or pretend to be a David Bowie expert. I'm no Kevin Cann or Nicholas Pegg, nor am I Mark Adams or Paul Kinder, and I'm sure there are fans out there who have probably forgotten more about David Bowie than I will ever know. That said, I am a huge fan and I've enjoyed compiling these trivia questions into a book which I hope can be, at least of some interest, to David Bowie fans everywhere.

BEFORE STARTING . . .

Questions referencing release dates are generally UK release dates unless otherwise stated. Single questions are separated by blank lines but where there are two or more 'related' questions, these are presented in blocks. As an example, if the answer to a question is the name of a studio album release, there then follows a block of ten questions all about that particular album. In the first draft of the book, one of the ten questions about the album, concerned song lyrics. I had included the type of question that you tend to find, and indeed would expect to find, in your typical music quiz book, and that is:-

> Q. Identify the track from the following lyrics:
> ****************************
> ****************************

Unfortunately, there are many websites and legal experts out there who suggest using and printing lyrics in this way should be avoided at all costs, without having the appropriate permissions granted from the copyright owner to do so. Accordingly, I did email the publishers but they failed to respond. Risking prosecution is not something to be taken lightly and entering into any sort of litigation is a losing proposition. In the circumstances, therefore, I reluctantly took the difficult decision to remove all questions quoting one or two full lines of song lyrics.

The following type stylization is used in the book:-

Within both the Questions and Answers sections:-
- Albums and Music Video Films are in **bold.**
  Albums:- **Diamond Dogs, Tonight, Reality**
  Music films:- **A Reality Tour, Jazzin' For Blue Jean**

- Tracks are in *italics.*
  Tracks:- *Diamond Dogs, Tonight, Reality*

Additionally, within the Questions sections only, single quotes have been used for emphasis:-
- Books: 'At the Birth of Bowie', 'Free Spirit'
- Events: 'Fashion Rocks Awards', 'Brit Awards'
- Films: 'Basquiat', 'The Hunger'
- Radio Shows: 'Sounds of the 70s', 'Top Gear'
- Stage Plays: 'Lazarus', 'Pierrot In Turquoise'
- Tours: 'Serious Moonlight', 'Ziggy Stardust'
- TV Shows: 'Later with Jools', 'Top of the Pops'

DAVID BOWIE

ALL MY ~~IDIOT~~ 1500 QUESTIONS

ALL MY ~~IDIOT~~ 1500 QUESTIONS

pre 1960s

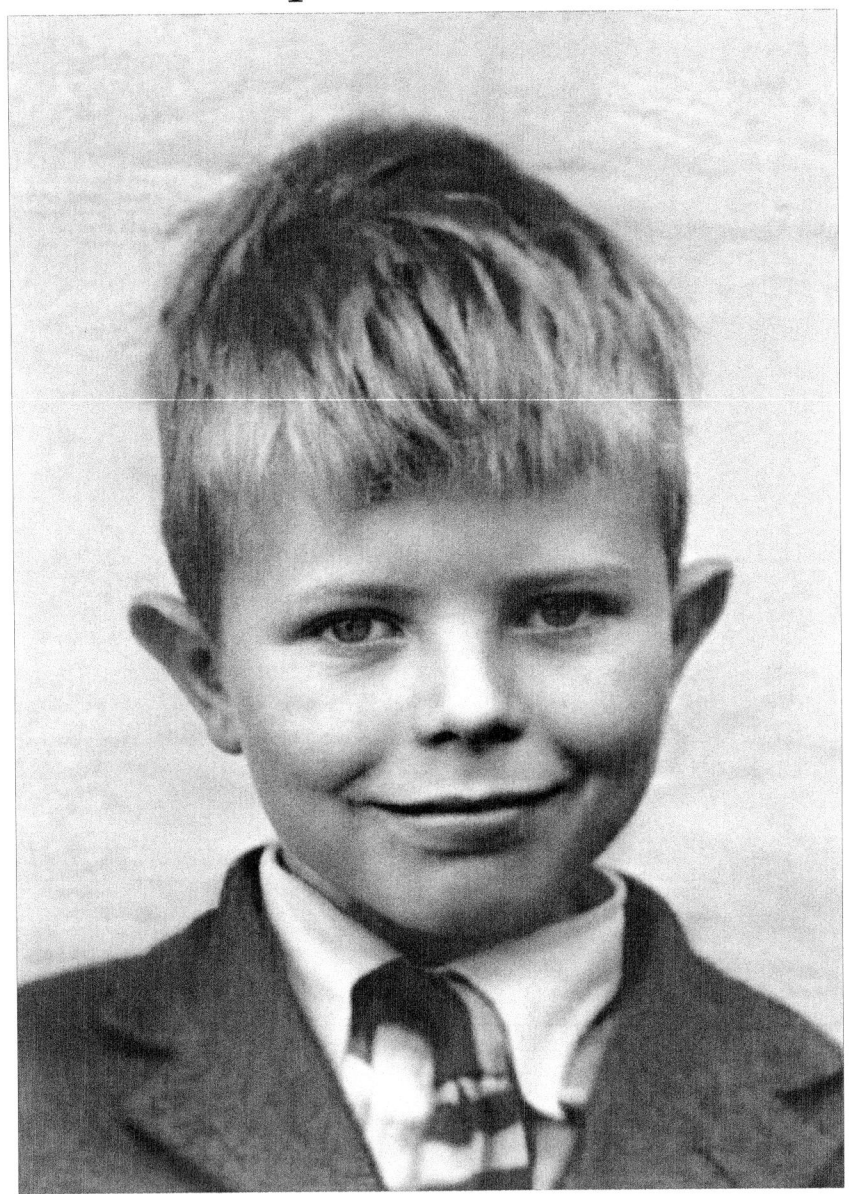

Figure 2: Alamy Stock Photo

pre 1960s
64 Questions

1. Born in 1882, what was the name of David's paternal grandfather?

2. Born in 1884, what was the name of David's maternal grandmother?

3. Born in 1887, what was the name of David's paternal grandmother?

4. Born in 1887, what was the name of David's maternal grandfather?

5. What was David's father's name?
6. He was born on the 21st November, of which year?
7. He was born at 41 Sepulchre Gate, in which Yorkshire town?
8. By what name was he known to family and friends?
9. Name his only sister, born two years earlier.

ALL MY ~~IDIOT~~ 1500 QUESTIONS

10. What was David's mother's name?
11. She was born on the 2nd October, of which year?
12. What was the name of the hospital near Folkestone where she was born?
13. She grew up at 15 Meadow Road, in which Kent town?
14. By what name was she known to family and friends?
15. The eldest of six children, she had four sisters, namely Victoria Honoria, Una Beatrix, Eileen Patricia and Vivienne May. What was the name of her only brother?

16. David's father's first marriage took place on the 19th December, of which year?
17. What was the name of his first wife?

18. David's father used most of a £3000 inheritance money he received, in 1933, trying to make a name for himself in showbiz and he particularly tried to bankroll the cabaret singing career of his wife. Under what stage name was his wife performing?
19. When the venture failed, what was the name of the club in London that David's father bought with the remainder of the inheritance? It was also destined for failure.

20. In 1937, David's mother gave birth to a son, someone who would later have a great influence on the young David. What was his name?
21. On what date was he born? (his second name is a clue)
22. Who was his father?

pre 1960s

23. What was the name of the daughter born in January 1938 to David's father and the unknown birth mother with whom he'd had a brief affair in Birmingham?

24. This daughter grew up, allegedly married an Egyptian businessman and then changed her name, coincidently to what?

25. In 1943, David's mother gave birth to a daughter (unknown birth father). She was put up for adoption but what was her name?

26. Born in Brooklyn, New York, in April 1944, who would go on to become a close personal friend of David's, producing much of his work throughout his career?

27. Having served in North Africa during the Second World War, David's father returned home to work for which organisation as a Public Relations Officer?

28. In 1946, David's mother first met his father, when she was working as a waitress at the Ritz cinema cafe, in which town?

29. On what date was David born?
30. At what address was David born?
31. What was David's full name?
32. Which American future rock 'n' roll star was celebrating his 12th birthday back home in Memphis, Tennessee, the exact same day that David was born?

33. James Newell Osterberg was born in April 1947. He was to become a close friend and collaborator of David's, but by what name is he better known?

34. On what date did David's parents marry?
35. Where did they get married?

36. September 1947 saw the birth of Marc Feld, someone who would later feature prominently in the early years of David's story. By what name did he become better known?

37. Which future member of Roxy Music was born in the village of Melton in Suffolk, in May 1948? He would go on to become David's friend and collaborator.

38. The future first Mrs. Jones/Bowie, Angie, was born in September 1949. In which country was she born?
39. What is her full name?

40. Carlos Alomar was born in May 1951 and he would become best known over the years for the work he did with David. In which country was Carlos born?

41. David's family lived in the house in which he was born, for the first six years of his life. Which school, within easy walking distance of the house, did David first attend in 1951?

42. As a young boy in 1952, whilst visiting his uncle's farm in Yorkshire, David attended a local agricultural show and inadvertently wandered close to which

dignitary, who commented "Oh hello little boy"? The incident was reported in the local newspaper.

43. Frank Madeloni was born in Brooklyn, New York in October 1952, and he would go on to work extensively with David throughout his career. By what name is Frank better known?

44. Which musical film starring Danny Kaye, and said to be pivotal in David's early years, was first released in the US, in November 1952?

45. Which song in the film was particularly important to David, commenting in later life that he loved the nursery rhyme feel to the tune?

46. Which house move did the Jones family undertake at the beginning of 1953?

47. Which infants school did David next attend, between 1953 and 1955?

48. To where did the family move home, just a year or so later, in 1954?

49. 1955 saw yet another family house move, but this time, the house would remain their home for the next ten years or more. What was the address of the new family home?

50. Which junior school did David then attend for the next three years, 1955 – 1958?

ALL MY ~~IDIOT~~ 1500 QUESTIONS

51. What is the name of the lifelong friend David met at school, whose own stage name would become Warren Peace?

52. In his final year at the junior school, David became a member of which school sports team?

53. David's future second wife, Iman, was born on the 25th July, of which year?
54. What is her full name?
55. In which country was she born?

56. On hearing which song by which American artist, released in October 1955, did David comment in future interviews, "I had heard God"?

57. What is the name of David's cousin who introduced him, with great effect, to the American stars of the 1950s such as Elvis Presley and Bill Haley? This cousin would later appear in a 2019 BBC documentary about David.

58. David and his cousin were taken by his father, in 1956, to see which all round entertainer, at the Finsbury Park Empire, going backstage afterwards to get autographs? The event had a huge influence on David and on his desire to become a star one day himself.

59. By 1957, who had David met at the 18th Bromley Wolf Cub Scout Group, forming another lifelong

friendship? His own stage name for a short while would become Calvin James.

60. In 1958, David got to attend his preferred choice of secondary school. What was the name of that school?
61. By what name is that secondary school now known, having merged with other art schools in the area, back in the early 1960s?

62. In 1958, David made his first musical public performance at a scout summer camp with friends, but where was it?

63. By the end of the decade, David had been given a copy of the book 'On the Road' and has since commented on how it proved to be a turning point in his life. Who gave him the copy of the book?
64. Who wrote the book?

Figure 3: Author's Photos, the pre 1960s houses

pre 1960s
64 Answers

1. Robert Haywood Jones
2. Margaret Alice Heaton
3. Zillah Hannah Blackburn
4. James Edward Burns
5. Haywood Stenton Jones
6. 1912
7. Doncaster
8. John
9. Roma
10. Margaret Mary Burns
11. 1913
12. Shorncliffe Army Camp Hospital
13. Southborough in the wider borough of Tunbridge Wells
14. Peggy
15. James Swetenham
16. 1933
17. Hilda Louise Sullivan
18. The Viennese Nightingale

ALL MY ~~IDIOT~~ 1500 QUESTIONS

19. The Boop A Doop Club
20. Terence Guy Adair Burns
21. 5th November 1937
22. Jack Isaac 'Wolf' Rosenberg
23. Annette Jones
24. Iman
25. Myra Ann Burns
26. Tony Visconti
27. Dr. Barnardo's
28. Tunbridge Wells
29. 8th January 1947 (a Wednesday)
30. 40 Stansfield Road, Brixton
31. David Robert Jones
32. Elvis Presley
33. Iggy Pop
34. 12th September 1947
35. Brixton Registry Office
36. Marc Bolan
37. Brian Eno (His confirmation name is derived from the Catholic grammar school he attended in 1959, taking the name Brian Peter George St. John le Baptiste de la Salle Eno)
38. Cyprus
39. Mary Angela Barnett
40. Puerto Rico
41. Stockwell Primary School, Brixton
42. The Queen
43. Earl Slick
44. Hans Christian Anderson
45. *Inchworm*
46. 106 Canon Road, Bromley
47. Raglan Infants School, Bromley

pre 1960s

48. 23 Clarence Road, Bromley
49. 4 Plaistow Grove, Sundridge Park, Bromley
50. Burnt Ash Junior School, Bromley
51. Geoff MacCormack
52. The football team
53. 1955
54. Zara Mohamed Abdulmajid
55. Somalia
56. *Tutti Frutti* by Little Richard
57. Kristina Paulsen (now Kristina Amadeus)
58. Tommy Steele
59. George Underwood
60. Bromley Technical High School
61. Ravens Wood School
62. Corf Campsite, near Shalfleet, on the Isle Of Wight
63. David's half-brother, Terry
64. Jack Kerouac

Figure 4: Author's Photos, the pre 1960s schools

ALL MY ~~IDIOT~~ 1500 QUESTIONS

the 1960s

Figure 5: Alamy Stock Photo

the 1960s
168 Questions

65. In February 1962, whilst still at school, David's left eye was damaged in a fight with which lifelong friend?
66. The fight was over a girl. What was her name?
67. Name the school's head teacher who personally took David to the Farnborough Hospital for treatment.

68. Who was David's inspirational art teacher at Bromley Technical High School?

69. Who was David's music teacher at Bromley Technical High School?

70. Who, in the spring of 1962, did David contact to ask if he would teach him to play the saxophone?

ALL MY ~~IDIOT~~ 1500 QUESTIONS

71. David was also learning to play guitar in the early 1960s. True or False, David was naturally left handed but played the guitar right handed!

72. What was the name of the first band David joined, in June 1962?

73. David started to experiment with different stage names. By what name had he become known by the end of 1962?

74. Which of the following musicians was NOT a member of the band?
    a) Neville Wills
    b) George Underwood
    c) Dave Crook
    d) Roger Bluck

75. Was Alan Dodds the guitarist or the drummer?

76. By the start of 1963, which two female backing singers had joined the band?

77. In whose record shop did David take up a Saturday job for a short while, around May 1963?

78. David left school in July 1963 with one 'O' Level, in which subject?

79. On leaving school in 1963, at which commercial art studio did David take his first job as Junior Visualizer?

80. What was the title of the song co-written by David, which was recorded in August 1963? It's said to be the only studio recording of The Konrads, which

featured Roger Ferris on lead vocal, and David on harmonies.

81. Who were The Hooker Brothers, having originally gone by the name of Dave's Reds and Blues?

82. At the beginning of which year did David join his second band, The King Bees?
83. By what stage name was David now known?
84. Which of these King Bees, played drums?
    a) Robert Allen
    b) Roger Bluck
    c) Dave Howard
    d) George Underwood

85. What was the name of the business tycoon to whom David wrote a letter, in March 1964, asking for financial help for The King Bees?

86. Who became David's first manager, in April 1964?

87. David released his first single with The King Bees in June 1964. Name both the A side and the B side of the single.
88. On which Decca subsidiary label was the record released?
89. To which of these names was the record credited?
    a) The King Bees
    b) The King Bees featuring Davy Jones
    c) Dave Jay and The King Bees
    d) Davie Jones with The King Bees

ALL MY ~~IDIOT~~ 1500 QUESTIONS

90. On which BBC TV show, in June 1964, did *Liza Jane* feature? The panel voted it a 'Miss' (as opposed to a 'Hit')

91. Which other budding young artist did David meet for the first time, in July 1964, whilst they were both painting the walls of Leslie Conn's Denmark Street office? They were soon to become friends and musical rivals.

92. David joined his third band in July 1964, an outfit from Maidstone. Name the band.
93. Which one of the following musicians was in the band?
    a) Denis Taylor
    b) Bob Solly
    c) Graham Rivens
    d) Derek Boyes
94. Who played bass guitar, John Watson or Mick White?
95. As well as David, which two other band members played saxophone?

96. Who became David's girlfriend for a while, in November 1964, after watching him perform at The Marquee? Two years earlier, in 1962, she had become the British Junior Water Skiing Champion.

97. David and friends appeared on the 'Tonight' TV programme in November 1964, having formed 'The Society' for what?
98. Who interviewed David on the show?

the 1960s

99. In January 1965, one of David's own compositions appeared on vinyl for the very first time. *Take My Tip* was released as the B side of the single *Restless*, by which American actor?

100. In March 1965 on the Parlophone record label, *I Pity The Fool* became the first single to be released by David and The Manish Boys. Which of David's own compositions was on the B side?
101. To whom was the single credited?
102. Which session musician, and future founder of Led Zeppelin, played guitar on the single?
103. Who produced the single?

104. David and The Manish Boys appeared on the TV show 'Gadzooks! It's All Happening', in March 1965. Which track did they perform?

105. Which of David's close friends released a single in April 1965, on the Columbia record label, entitled *Some Things You Never Get Used To*?

106. David and many other musicians and friends were, by the mid-1960s, regularly meeting up at La Gioconda Coffee Bar. In which London street was the coffee bar situated?
107. By what other name was the street known?

108. What was the name of the next band David joined, in May 1965?
109. From where on the South East coast did the band originate?

110. Les Mighall was the original drummer in the band. Who eventually replaced him?
111. Who were the other two members of the band?
112. Partly down to a lack of money, in what type of vehicle would the band often sleep, and travel to gigs?

113. Who became David's second manager, just for a short while, in July 1965?

114. The first single with the new band was released in August 1965. Name both the A side and the B side, both songs being David's own compositions.
115. On which record label was the single released?
116. Who, as seen on the vinyl label itself, was credited as the artist?
117. Who produced the single?

118. Although David himself chose the name 'Bowie', who was it who suggested to his manager Ralph Horton in September 1965, that he changed his name? He subsequently became David's third manager.
119. What was the main reason for changing his name?
120. Which 19th century American pioneer was the inspiration for the name change?

121. *Steamship Taro* is an anagram of which lesser known song written by David, around September 1965?

122. David signed to Pye records in November 1965. Which record producer signed him to the record label?

the 1960s

123. The first Pye single released in January 1966, was also the first to feature the name 'David Bowie'. The B side was *And I Say To Myself*, what was the A side?
124. To which of the following was the single credited?
    a) David Bowie
    b) David Bowie with The Lower Third
    c) The Lower Third and David Bowie
    d) David Bowie's Lower Third

125. What was the name of David's next band, a backing band, formed in February 1966?
126. Complete the band members names:-
    a) J _ _ _ H _ _ _ _ _ _ _ _ _ (Guitar)
    b) D _ _ _ _ F _ _ _ _ _ _ _ (Bass)
    c) J _ _ _ E _ _ _ _ (Drums)
    d) D _ _ _ _ B _ _ _ _ (Keyboards)

127. In March 1966, David and the band appeared on which TV pop music show, performing *Can't Help Thinking About Me*?

128. Name both sides of the next Pye single, released in April 1966.
129. To whom was the single credited?

130. In April 1966, Ken Pitt agreed with Ralph Horton to co-manage David, and witnessed him enjoying a nine week residency at The Marquee. By what name was The Marquee residency billed?

ALL MY ~~IDIOT~~ 1500 QUESTIONS

131. John 'Hutch' Hutchinson, the original guitar player in The Buzz, returned home to Scarborough in June 1966. Who replaced him on guitar?

132. The third and final single on the Pye record label was released in August 1966. *I Dig Everything* was the A side, what was the B side?

133. By the mid-1960s, whose cockney singing style, of Gurney Slade fame, was starting to have a big influence on David?

134. In an effort to get a recording contract for David in October 1966, Ken Pitt took copies of *Rubber Band*, *The London Boys* and *The Gravedigger* to Decca. To which head of promotion at the record label did Ken play *Rubber Band*?

135. David signed to the Decca subsidiary label, Deram, in October 1966. What was the first single released by David on the new label, in December of that year? The B side was *The London Boys*.

136. Which publishing company was, by the end of 1966, representing David?

137. Who at the publishing company, had signed the contract with Ralph Horton?

138. Who, in December 1966, returned home from the United States with a present for David, an acetate copy of the yet unreleased **The Velvet Underground & Nico**, given to him personally by Andy Warhol? It

the 1960s

proved to have a profound effect on David and became a treasured possession.

139. Paul Nicholas released one of David's songs as a single, in January 1967. What was Paul's stage name at the time?
140. What was the song?

141. In between projects, in the spring of 1967, David made unofficial ad-hoc appearances with which of these bands?
    a) The Fashion Squad
    b) The Blazin' Squad
    c) The Riot Squad
    d) The Goon Squad
142. Whilst with the band, David recorded a version of *Little Toy Soldier*, a sound effects-laden song with a similar musical arrangement to, and lifted lyrics from, which Velvet Underground track?

143. *The Laughing Gnome* was released as a single, in April 1967, on the Deram record label. What was the B side?

144. Who became David's sole manager, in April 1967?

145. Name David's 1st studio album, released in June 1967, on the Deram record label.
146. Which track opened the album?
147. Which track on the album expressed David's growing interest in Buddhism?

ALL MY ~~IDIOT~~ 1500 QUESTIONS

148. Misguided or planned release date, but which Beatles album was released at the same time?
149. Who produced the album?
150. Solve the following anagrams to identify the two album tracks:-
    a) *Dilbert Baltimore*
    b) *The Glass Demos*
151. Rather than hire a professional music arranger, which Buzz member, together with David, studied orchestral arrangements in an attempt to produce the scores themselves?
152. Which British conductor ultimately assisted with the orchestral arrangements?
153. Which track consisted wholly of sound effects rather than instruments?
154. Who took the album cover photo of David?
155. Johnny, Molly and Arthur, all appeared in which track?

156. Released as a single in July 1967, on the Deram record label, the B side was *Did You Ever Have A Dream*. What was the A side?
157. Which 'go to' session musician contributed banjo to the track *Did You Ever Have A Dream*?

158. By July 1967, David's interest in Tibet had grown, Buddhism had become an attractive prospect, and he even considered becoming a Buddhist Monk. What was the name of the Buddhist monk who became David's teacher and friend, having himself escaped the Chinese invasion of Tibet in 1959? He arrived in the UK in 1965.

the 1960s

159. Hull born singer Ronnie Hilton, released the single *If I Were A Rich Man* from the 'Fiddler On The Roof' musical, in July 1967. Which of David's songs did he cover for the B side?

160. With which London mime artist did David become friends, having attended one of his shows (Clowns Hour) in August 1967, and heard his own debut album being played during the interval?

161. Made by Border Films and filmed in September 1967, what was the name of the short film by Michael Armstrong in which David appeared?
162. What was the name of David's character?
163. Which actor played the part of the artist?

164. In September 1967 and December 1967 respectively, two bands (The Slender Party and The Beatstalkers) each recorded and released their own version of one of David's songs. Which song?

165. David recorded many sessions for BBC Radio in the late 1960s and early 1970s. Commissioned and produced by Bernie Andrews, what was the name of the Radio One pop music programme for which David recorded his first session, in December 1967? It was broadcast a few days later on Christmas Eve.

166. Premiered at the Oxford New Theatre, in December 1967, what was the title of Lindsay Kemp's stage production in which David appeared?

ALL MY ~~IDIOT~~ 1500 QUESTIONS

167. Which character did David play?
168. Which character was played by Jack Birkett?
169. Who designed David's costume (she would go on to work with David again in the future)?

170. In January 1968, David took part in the recording of a dance minuet for which BBC TV production? It was broadcast in May 1968.
171. Who was the beautiful young dancer also in the cast, with whom David ultimately fell in love?

172. In February 1968, David wrote a set of lyrics to a French tune by Claude François, called *Comme D'Habitude*. What did David call his version of the song?
173. Legendary US songwriter Paul Anka wrote a second set of lyrics for the same tune. Released by Frank Sinatra a year later, what had Anka called his version of the song?

174. What was the name of the mini rock opera that David penned in February 1968, but which was never released?

175. Which 1960s pop star released a version of David's *Silly Boy Blue* as the B side to his single *One Minute Woman*, in March 1968, on the Parlophone record label?

176. In May 1968, David recorded a second session for BBC Radio One's 'Top Gear' programme, performing

the 1960s

five early tracks. Which Radio One DJ presented the programme?

177. In May 1968, David performed at a charity event, the 'Fantastic Gandalf's Garden Magical Sunday', in Covent Garden. He performed a twenty minute Tibetan mime, set to music which included which one of his own compositions?
178. Which act was Top of the Bill at the event?
179. Which Radio One DJ compared the show?

180. With whom was David living, around August 1968, at 22 Clareville Grove in South Kensington?

181. Who, along with David and Hermione, in September 1968, formed a mixed media trio performing mime, poetry, music and dance?
182. Debuting at The Roundhouse in September 1968, by what name was the trio known?
183. Who, by November 1968, had replaced Tony Hill in the trio?
184. With the change of personnel came a change of name too. By what name was the new trio known?

185. The Beatstalkers released their single *Little Boy* in January 1969, with yet another of David's songs on the B side. Which song?

186. Filmed on a double decker bus in black and white, which ice cream did David advertise in January 1969?

27

ALL MY ~~IDIOT~~ 1500 QUESTIONS

187. Filmed in January and February 1969 (but not officially released until 1984), what was the name of the 30 minute promotional film designed to showcase David's talents, and financed by Ken Pitt?
188. The film featured some of David's early songs but which new song did David compose in response to Pitt's request to write something new, specifically for the promotion?
189. Which Stanley Kubrick film had David recently seen, inspiring him to write the new song?
190. What was the name of the mime piece that David performed in the film?
191. Which song featured David, Hermione and 'Hutch' sitting on cushions, with Hermione and 'Hutch' sharing lead vocals?
192. In which song did David pay homage to the tobacco spitting exploits of his Grandfather Jones?
193. Who directed the film?

194. In January 1969, David recorded German versions of which two songs? The German titles were *Mit In Deinem Traum* and *Liebe Dich Bis Dienstag*, respectively.

195. For which musical did David audition unsuccessfully, at The Shaftesbury Theatre in London, in February 1969?

196. By early 1969, Hermione had left David for Scandinavia where she had been offered a part in which film?

the 1960s

197. In March 1969, David moved into the flat belonging to his friend Barrie Jackson and his wife Christina, at 24 Foxgrove Road in Beckenham. Just a few weeks later, he had moved into the lower floor Flat 1, at the same address. Who was living there, subsequently becoming his lover as well as his landlady?

198. David met future wife Angie, at a King Crimson show at the Speakeasy club in London's West End, in April 1969. Which mutual friend introduced them?

199. In May 1969, at which Beckenham High Street pub did David and Mary Finnigan set up a regular weekly folk club, ultimately morphing into what became a successful Arts Lab?

200. To which record label did David sign, in June 1969?

201. July 1969 saw the release of David's biggest single to date, *Space Oddity*. Which track was on the B side?

202. Tony Visconti turned down the offer to produce the *Space Oddity* track on the grounds that he didn't like it, and called it a 'novelty' song. Who produced the track in his place?

203. In which two countries did David attend song festivals in July 1969?

204. At which one of these festivals did David receive an award for best produced record?

205. Which of his own compositions did David perform at both festivals?

ALL MY ~~IDIOT~~ 1500 QUESTIONS

206. Who died of pneumonia on the 5th August 1969, causing David great pain and distress?

207. The Growth Arts Lab culminated in an open air Free Festival performed on the 16th August 1969. Where did the festival take place?
208. Who cooked hamburgers in a wheelbarrow?
209. Who performed a duet with David, a reggae version of *Space Oddity*?
210. Which track on the upcoming new album did David write about the festival?

211. As David's involvement with the Arts Lab came to an end, who stepped in on several occasions to fill the gap, and in doing so formed an early, tentative, Cockney Rebel?

212. What was the name of the Victorian building into which David and Angie moved, in the summer of 1969?
213. What was the full address of their ground floor flat dwelling?
214. Who were living in the basement before it was ultimately converted into a recording studio?

215. In which film based on the novel by Leslie Thomas, did David appear briefly as an extra (blink and you miss him), when released in October 1969?

216. On whose show, in October 1969, did David make his last BBC Radio One appearance of the decade? Backed by Junior's Eyes, he performed the three

the 1960s

songs, *Unwashed And Somewhat Slightly Dazed*, *Let Me Sleep Beside You* and *Janine*.

217. Name David's 2nd studio album, released in November 1969, on the Philips record label.
218. At which studios in London was the album recorded?
219. What name was given to the album release in the US?
220. Who played the mellotron on the album?
221. Solve the following anagrams to identify the two album tracks:-
    a) *Dogwood Smoking*
    b) *ICC Getty Memento*
222. Who played harmonica on *Unwashed And Somewhat Slightly Dazed?*
223. Having just finished working with The Beatles, who engineered the album?
224. David's ex-girlfriend Hermione Farthingale, was the subject of which two tracks?
225. Which track is said to have been written about George Underwood's girlfriend at the time?
226. Which British photographer took the portrait shot of David that appeared on the album cover?
227. Alongside Mick Wayne, Tim Renwick and John Lodge, who was the fourth member of the band Junior's Eyes, who played on the album?

228. At which London Palladium charity event in November 1969, did David appear performing *Space Oddity* and *Wild Eyed Boy From Freecloud?*
229. Which member of the Royal Family was in attendance?

ALL MY ~~IDIOT~~ 1500 QUESTIONS

230. In December 1969, David started work on an Italian version of *Space Oddity*. What was the title of the Italian version?

231. To what does the Italian title translate back into English?

232. By the end of the 1960s, David's half-brother Terry, was suffering from schizophrenia and was a regular voluntary patient at which mental institution in the London Borough of Croydon?

Figure 6: Selection of items from Author's Collection, featuring works from, and recollections of, the 1960s

the 1960s
168 Answers

65. George Underwood
66. Carol Goldsmith
67. Frederick French
68. Owen Frampton
69. Brian Lane
70. Ronnie Ross
71. It's true
72. The Konrads
73. Dave Jay
74. d) Roger Bluck
75. Alan was the guitarist
76. Stella and Christine Patton
77. Vic Furlong's Record Shop
78. Art
79. Nevin D Hirst Advertising Agency
80. *I Never Dreamed*
81. A side project trio put together by David, consisting of himself, George Underwood and Viv Andrews

82. 1964
83. Davie Jones
84. a) Robert Allen
85. John Bloom
86. Leslie Conn
87. *Liza Jane / Louie, Louie Go Home*
88. Vocalion Pop
89. d) Davie Jones with The King Bees
90. Juke Box Jury
91. Marc Bolan
92. The Manish Boys
93. b) Bob Solly
94. John Watson (Mick White played drums)
95. Woolf Byrne and Paul Rodriguez
96. Dana Gillespie
97. The Society For The Prevention Of Cruelty To Long Haired Men
98. Cliff Michelmore
99. Kenny Miller
100. *Take My Tip*
101. The Manish Boys (no separate credit for David)
102. Jimmy Page
103. Shel Talmy
104. *I Pity The Fool*
105. Calvin James (aka George Underwood)
106. Denmark Street
107. Tin Pan Alley
108. The Lower Third
109. Margate
110. Phil Lancaster
111. Denis Taylor and Graham Rivens
112. An old ambulance

the 1960s

113. Ralph Horton
114. *You've Got A Habit Of Leaving / Baby Loves That Way*
115. Parlophone
116. Davy Jones (no mention of The Lower Third – and notice the subtle spelling difference now in his stage name, Davy rather than Davie)
117. Shel Talmy
118. Ken Pitt
119. There was already a Davy Jones making a name for himself playing the role of the Artful Dodger in the 'Oliver' musical on Broadway. He would later become a member of the successful pop band, The Monkees.
120. Jim Bowie
121. *That's A Promise*
122. Tony Hatch
123. *Can't Help Thinking About Me*
124. b) David Bowie with The Lower Third
125. The Buzz
126. a) John Hutchinson
    b) Derek Fearnley
    c) John Eager
    d) Derek Boyes
127. Ready Steady Go
128. *Do Anything You Say / Good Morning Girl*
129. David Bowie (David Bowie's first solo credited single)
130. The Bowie Showboat
131. Billy Gray
132. *I'm Not Losing Sleep*
133. Anthony Newley
134. Tony Hall (who then played it to Hugh Mendl)
135. *Rubber Band*

136. Essex Music International
137. David Platz
138. Ken Pitt
139. Oscar
140. *Over The Wall We Go*
141. c) The Riot Squad
142. *Venus In Furs*
143. *The Gospel According To Tony Day*
144. Ken Pitt
145. **David Bowie**
146. *Uncle Arthur*
147. *Silly Boy Blue*
148. **Sgt. Pepper's Lonely Hearts Club Band**
149. Mike Vernon
150. a) *Little Bombardier*
    b) *She's Got Medals*
151. Derek Fearnley (Dek)
152. Arthur Greenslade
153. *Please Mr. Gravedigger*
154. Gerald Fearnley (Dek's brother)
155. *Join The Gang*
156. *Love You Till Tuesday*
157. Big Jim Sullivan
158. Lama Chime Youngdong Rinpoche
159. *The Laughing Gnome*
160. Lindsay Kemp
161. The Image
162. The Boy
163. Michael Byrne
164. *Silver Treetop School For Boys*
165. Top Gear
166. Pierrot In Turquoise

167. Cloud
168. Harlequin
169. Natasha Kornilof
170. The Pistol Shot
171. Hermione Farthingale
172. *Even A Fool Learns To Love*
173. *My Way*
174. Ernie Johnson
175. Billy Fury
176. John Peel
177. *Silly Boy Blue*
178. Marc Bolan's Tyrannosaurus Rex
179. John Peel
180. Hermione Farthingale
181. Tony Hill
182. Turquoise
183. John 'Hutch' Hutchinson
184. Feathers
185. *When I'm Five*
186. Lyons Maid 'Luv' ice cream
187. **Love You Till Tuesday**
188. *Space Oddity*
189. 2001: A Space Odyssey
190. *The Mask*
191. *Ching-a-Ling*
192. *When I'm Five*
193. Malcolm J Thomson
194. *When I Live My Dream* and *Love You Till Tuesday*
195. Hair
196. Song Of Norway
197. Mary Finnigan

198. American A&R man with Mercury Records, Calvin Mark Lee
199. The Three Tuns
200. Mercury / Philips (Mercury for US and Philips for EU distributions respectively)
201. *Wild Eyed Boy From Freecloud*
202. Gus Dudgeon
203. Malta and Italy
204. The Italian Festival
205. *When I Live My Dream*
206. David's father, Haywood Stenton Jones (John)
207. Croydon Recreation Ground, Beckenham
208. David's girlfriend, Angie
209. Tony Visconti
210. *Memory Of A Free Festival*
211. Steve Harley
212. Haddon Hall
213. Flat 7, 42 Southend Road, Beckenham
214. Sue and Tony Frost (Sue, a seamstress, later assisted with costume creations and Tony became one of David's bodyguards)
215. The Virgin Soldiers
216. Dave Lee Travis
217. **David Bowie**
218. Trident Studios
219. The album had been re-titled **Man of Words, Man Of Music** for the US release. It's worth noting, however, that according to Cann, the text was added to the album sleeve to describe the artist and it was never intended to be the title of the album.
220. Rick Wakeman
221. *a) God Knows I'm Good*

b) Cygnet Committee
222. Benny Marshall
223. Ken Scott
224. Letter To Hermione and *An Occasional Dream*
225. Janine
226. Vernon Dewhurst
227. John Cambridge
228. Save Rave
229. Princess Margaret
230. Ragazzo Solo, Ragazza Sola
231. Lonely Boy, Lonely Girl
232. Cane Hill Hospital

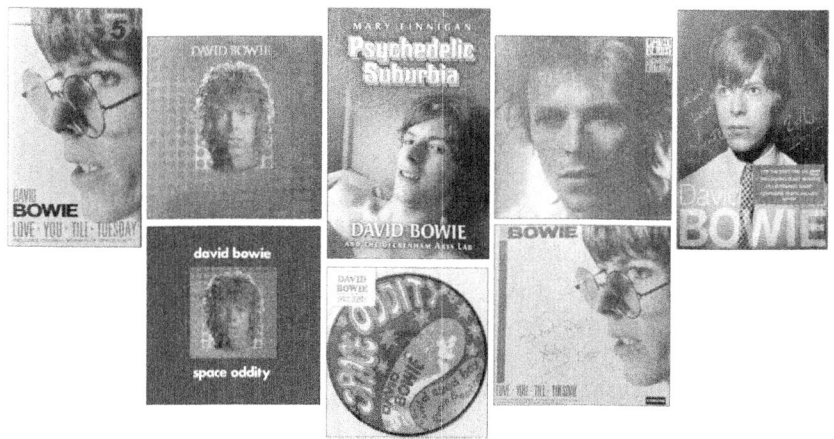

Figure 7: Selection of items from Author's Collection, featuring works from, and recollections of, the 1960s

ALL MY ~~IDIOT~~ 1500 QUESTIONS

the 1970s

Figure 8: Alamy Stock Photo

the 1970s
373 Questions

233. In January 1970, David worked once more with Lindsay Kemp on a new adaptation of 'Pierrot In Turquoise', for performances in Edinburgh. Which two new songs did David write for the production?
234. At Kemp's request, David also penned new lyrics for his *London Bye Ta Ta* track. What did the track become?
235. Which other track, Kemp's favourite, was also used in the production, both at the beginning and at the end?
236. By what name had the production become known when it was broadcast on Scottish TV in July 1970?

237. In February 1970, David met a guitarist from Hull, someone who would feature prominently in David's rise to stardom. What was his name?

238. On which BBC Radio One programme, introduced by John Peel, did David appear in February 1970? The

setlist was the most comprehensive to date and featured Mick Ronson working with David for the first time, having met just a few days earlier.

239. What was the name of the band that David formed in February 1970?
240. Who were the other three members of the band?
241. Angie and Tony Visconti's girlfriend at the time, made costumes for the band members, specifically for a February 1970 gig at The Roundhouse, which many regard as the birth of 'glam'. Who was Visconti's girlfriend at the time?
242. Match the band members to the following costumed characters :-
    a) Cowboyman
    b) Gangsterman
    c) Hypeman
    d) Rainbowman

243. Which song about Angie was released as a single, in March 1970 on the Mercury record label?
244. Which of David's friends played lead guitar on the single?

245. Which record company released **The World Of David Bowie** album, in March 1970?

246. On what date did David and Angie marry?
247. Where did they get married?
248. Which two friends were the intended witnesses to the marriage?

the 1970s

249. Who, without warning, replaced one of the witnesses at the last minute?
250. What did David and Angie exchange instead of the traditional wedding rings?

251. Recorded in March 1970 and broadcast in April 1970, David and the band appeared on Andy Ferris' BBC Radio One show, 'Sounds of the 70s', performing four tracks. By what collective name were Cambridge, Ronson and Visconti listed on the BBC contract?

252. At Mick Ronson's suggestion, who in April 1970, replaced John Cambridge on drums after John had struggled to play a 'tricky bit' in *The Supermen*?

253. Who did David meet in April 1970, promising to get him out of his current contract with Ken Pitt?
254. Who was the Head of Philips who had set up the meeting?

255. With which showbiz accountant did Tony Defries have a management company?
256. What was the name of the management company?

257. Which award did David receive in May 1970 for his composition, *Space Oddity*?

258. Which single, released in June 1970 on the Mercury record label, featured Mick Ronson for the first time?

ALL MY ~~IDIOT~~ 1500 QUESTIONS

259. As his publishing deal with Essex music came to an end, who was it who signed David to Chrysalis Music in October 1970?

260. Released in January 1971 on the Mercury record label, name both sides of the only single released that year.

261. To which country, in January 1971, did David embark on a publicity tour to promote his latest album, although no official live performances were allowed due to work visa restrictions?

262. Who from Mercury Records met David at the airport and oversaw the whole trip?

263. Whilst there, David saw one of the last performances of the Velvet Underground, at the Electric Circus in New York. David went backstage to talk to, who he thought was Lou Reed, but Lou had left the band some months earlier. To whom had David actually been talking?

264. In February 1971, David had plans for a new project, a new group called The Arnold Corns. Which fashion designer did David meet, exploring the possibility that he could become the group's frontman?

265. What stage name did this fashion designer adopt for his role in the group?

266. It turned out that the new frontman wasn't a singer so David's vocals were used instead. The first single released in May 1971 flopped and a second intended single was abandoned. Which four songs were recorded for the two singles?

the 1970s

267. What was the title of the song written by David, in April 1971, about his car, a 1932 Riley Gamecock?

268. In the spring of 1971, David penned a 'lesser known' song by the name of *How Lucky You Are*. By what other name, an earlier working title, was the track also known?

269. In 1971, Mercury released a compilation album by various artists entitled **Dimension Of Miracles**. Which one song from David was featured on the album?

270. Name David's 3rd studio album, released in April 1971, on the Mercury record label. It had already been released in the US a few months earlier.

271. Who, whilst working as a session musician in the mid-1960s, had given David the riff for *The Supermen*?

272. Solve the following anagrams to identify the two album tracks:-
 a) *Thelma Mandel*
 b) *Del Smokes Hooch*

273. Who played Moog synthesiser on the album?

274. At which Mayfair boutique in London, had David bought the man's dress, famously worn on the album cover photo?

275. For the US release, the cover artwork was a cartoon drawing of a cowboy based on John Wayne, stood in front of an asylum based on Cane Hill. Who designed the cartoon cover?

ALL MY ~~IDIOT~~ 1500 QUESTIONS

276. On which track did David rediscover the varispeed vocal techniques used a few years earlier on *The Laughing Gnome*?
277. What was the original title that David had intended for the album?
278. Who produced the album?
279. Which three track names all start with '*The*'?
280. Which Lebanese-American writer, poet and visual artist was namechecked in the opening track?

281. Released on the RAK record label in April 1971, who had a hit with David's newly written song, *Oh You Pretty Things*?
282. Who played piano on the 'Top of the Pops' performance of this single, a tape long lost by the BBC?

283. Which new music management company did Tony Defries register in May 1971?

284. Who, around May 1971, joined Mick Ronson and Mick 'Woody' Woodmansey in David's band, replacing Tony Visconti on bass?

285. David was listening to a Neil Young album when news came through that Angie had given birth to their son. On what date was their son born?
286. What is his full name?
287. Which song, that ended up on the next album, did David write to commemorate the birth?

288. On which BBC Radio One show, in June 1971, did Trevor Bolder first play with David, Ronson and Woodmansey? It was David's sixth BBC Radio One session.
289. Some of David's friends were also present and contributed vocals to the set. Who sang lead vocals on the track *Song For Bob Dylan*?
290. Who sang lead vocals on *Andy Warhol*? She would go on to release the track as a single herself, in 1974.

291. At which festival did David perform for the first time in June 1971, although he didn't get on stage until 5am, the morning after the evening he should have played?
292. Which other musician(s) accompanied David on stage?

293. To which famous actor, comedian, composer and musician from the 1960s did Defries write, in July 1971, requesting that he come play piano on tracks for David's upcoming new album?

294. In July 1971, Defries put together a promotional vinyl (**BOWPROMO**) featuring David on one side, and which artist on the other?
295. Armed with the promotional vinyl, with whom at RCA Records in August 1971, did Defries negotiate a recording contract for David?

296. Having already had a two week run in New York, which Andy Warhol play opened at the Roundhouse in London, in August 1971?

297. At which nearby venue did some of the cast go to see David perform for the first time?
298. Many of the cast, including Kathy Dorritie, ultimately went on to work for David and Defries. Which character did Kathy play in the production?
299. By what name is Kathy Dorritie better known?

300. David travelled to the US in September 1971 to sign the contract that Defries had negotiated with RCA. Whilst there, David got to meet Andy Warhol at The Factory and played the acetate of *Andy Warhol* to him. True or False, Andy loved it !

301. David's final BBC Radio One session of 1971, was for Bob Harris' 'Sounds of the 70s' show, in September 1971. Performing seven songs together, who was the only musician to accompany David?

302. Peter Noone's follow up single to *Oh You Pretty Things* was released on the RAK record label in October 1971, a song called *Walnut Whirl*. Which of David's songs was on the B side?

303. In October 1971, there was talk of David performing a duet with which English actor, famous for his many portrayals of Count Dracula in the Hammer Horror films? Nothing came of any such talk.

304. Tony Visconti had long left David's band to go work with Marc Bolan but which Eurovision Song Contest singer did Tony marry in November 1971?

the 1970s

305. Name David's 4th studio album, released in December 1971, the first one on the RCA record label.
306. Solve the following anagrams to identify the two album tracks:-
    a) *Brett Ashbey Howler*
    b) *Floyd Bronson Bag*
307. According to the rear cover sleeve notes, who produced the album?
308. On which track did Trevor Bolder play trumpet?
309. Which track on the album was 'inspired by Frankie'?
310. Which track was not written by David?
311. Which two friends and illustrators, designed and coloured the album cover, working from the original photos taken by Brian Ward?
312. Other than David, who else played piano on the album?
313. Clara appeared in which track?
314. In what way was the New Zealand version of the album cover, different and unique?
315. Against which track on the rear cover, did David write 'some V.U. White Light returned with thanks'?

316. *Changes* was released as a single, in January 1972, on the RCA record label but it was not a commercial success. Which BBC Radio One DJ, however, played it every day as his 'record of the week'?

317. By 1972, David had created his alter-ego character Ziggy Stardust, inspired in part at least, by Vince Taylor and Norman Carl Odam. By what name is Norman Carl Odam better known?

ALL MY ~~IDIOT~~ 1500 QUESTIONS

318. Who, as well as being Peggy Jones' regular hairdresser at the Evelyn Paget salon in Beckenham High Street, was responsible for giving David the famous 'Ziggy' cut? She ultimately went on tour as David's personal hairdresser and wardrobe assistant.

319. David performed two BBC Radio One sessions, just a week apart, in January 1972. The first session was recorded on the 11th January 1972 for 'Sounds of the 70s', and was introduced by which DJ?

320. The second session was recorded a week later on the 18th January 1972, again for 'Sounds of the 70s'. Which DJ presented the second show?

321. On each show, David performed new material intended for the next album, but he also included one track from **Hunky Dory**. Which track?

322. To whom, in an exclusive January 1972 interview, did David first announce his sexual ambiguity?

323. For which music paper was the interview conducted?

324. The first outing as the Ziggy Stardust character came in January 1972 at what is commonly regarded as the warm-up show for the first 'Ziggy Stardust' tour. Where was the warm-up gig held?

325. Which two members of future band Queen, were in the audience that night?

326. For which BBC TV show, presented by Richard Williams in February 1972, did David perform *Oh You Pretty Things*, *Queen Bitch* and *Five Years*?

the 1970s

327. Ziggy's second outing, the first show of the first 'Ziggy Stardust' tour, was held at which venue, in February 1972?

328. As well as the mainstay of the band, Bolder, Ronson and Woodmansey, who joined the band on keyboards for the tour?

329. The follow-up album was not far from completion but RCA's Dennis Katz wasn't sure there was an obvious track suitable for 'single' release. In direct response, which track did David go away to write? The new track would ultimately replace *Round And Round* on the new album.

330. In February 1972, David's half-brother Terry, married a fellow Cane Hill patient, at Croydon Registry Office. What was her name?

331. As the tour gathered pace, by what name did David's backing band of Bolder, Ronson and Woodmansey, become collectively known?

332. During 1972, David released three singles on the RCA record label, all of which charted. Listed here in alphabetical order, rearrange into the chronological order in which they were released.
    a) *John I'm Only Dancing*
    b) *Starman*
    c) *The Jean Genie*

333. The triple album **Glastonbury Fayre** was released in April 1972, on the Revelation record label. Although

51

David had actually performed at the 1971 event, he only contributed a studio version of which track?

334. David performed his final three BBC Radio One sessions, all in May 1972. Two performances were once again for the 'Sounds of the 70s' programme, introduced by John Peel and Bob Harris respectively. Sandwiched between the two, what was the name of the third programme for which David performed?

335. Name David's 5th studio album, released in June 1972, on the RCA record label.
336. What instructions as to how the album should be played, were printed on the rear cover sleeve?
337. In which London street, off Regent Street, did Brian Ward conduct the photoshoot for the album cover?
338. Whose Les Paul guitar was David holding for the photoshoot?
339. Solve the following anagrams to identify the two album tracks:-
    a) *Yoghurt Fools Anne*
    b) *Gratuity Effects*
340. The last track on Side One, *It Ain't Easy,* was not written by David. Who wrote it?
341. The inner sleeve showed photographs of David and the Spiders in 'droog' like poses, a reference to which film, cited by David as being a big inspiration for Ziggy?
342. Which friend and rival is thought to have been the key inspiration for the track *Lady Stardust?*
343. Who went to fight in Belfast?

the 1970s

344. Although not credited, which of David's ex-girlfriends contributed backing vocals on *It Ain't Easy?*
345. Which track closed the album?

346. On which children's TV show did David appear in June 1972, performing *Starman*, just a few days prior to the famous 'Top Of The Pops' performance in July?

347. As the 'Ziggy Stardust' tour kicked on, who became the tour's official photographer?
348. At which venue in June 1972, did the photographer famously first capture David simulating fellatio on Mick Ronson's guitar?
349. In which music magazine did Tony Defries take out a full page ad, showcasing the photo, with a view to further promoting David's career?

350. Which American Godfather of Shock Rock, did David, Iggy Pop and Mick Rock see perform at Wembley Empire Pool in June 1972? David was enthralled at the performance giving him the idea to work more theatrics into his own shows.

351. In June 1972, to what did Defries change the name of his Minnie Bell Music management company?

352. The famous 'Top Of The Pops' recording of David and the band performing *Starman* was broadcast by the BBC on 6th July 1972. The performance is now legendary and launched David to stardom. Who was seen on the broadcast, playing piano?

ALL MY ~~IDIOT~~ 1500 QUESTIONS

353. In July 1972, David appeared at The Royal Festival Hall, in aid of which charity?
354. Who introduced David to the stage, telling the audience that they were about to witness the second greatest thing to God?
355. Lou Reed joined David on stage to perform *White Light White Heat*, *Sweet Jane* and which other of Lou's songs?

356. Which of David's songs did Mott The Hoople record and release in July 1972, reviving their fortunes at a time when they were about to disband?

357. Recorded in August 1972 and released a few months later, which of Lou Reed's albums did David co-produce with Mick Ronson?
358. Which former saxophone teacher to David back in the early 1960s, contributed baritone saxophone to the track *Walk On The Wild Side*?

359. The second part of the first 'Ziggy Stardust' tour kicked off in August 1972, with two consecutive nights at which Finsbury Park theatre?
360. An elaborate stage design, a la 'The Living Theatre' art group performance of Frankenstein in the 1960s, was set up for the shows. Who, together with his dance troupe, The Astronettes, reconnected with David to work alongside him for those shows?
361. Which English rock band founded by Bryan Ferry, was the support act on both nights?
362. Which friend designed the programme for those shows?

the 1970s

363. David was the first act to play at the newly opened Hard Rock venue, in September 1972. In which English city was the concert theatre located?

364. In September 1972, how did David and Angie, together with George and Birgit Underwood, travel to the US for the American leg of the tour?

365. On singer/songwriter Annette Peacock's recommendation, who prior to the start of the American leg of the tour, joined David and the Spiders as keyboard player?

366. By the start of the first US tour in September 1972, which two bodyguards had been employed as personal security to David?

367. In which city in Ohio, did the American leg of the tour begin, in September 1972?

368. Which show in October 1972 was broadcast live by the KMET-FM radio station? The show became a popular bootleg and eventually received an official release in 2008.

369. In November 1972, which song did David write, having been inspired by the barren landscape between Seattle and Phoenix?

370. RCA re-issued the two Philips/Mercury albums in November 1972, with different album covers and each

included an up to date poster. Which of these albums had also been re-titled?

371. Which 40 second filler track from the original 1969 **David Bowie** album, had been omitted from the re-issue?

372. Having arrived home from the US, David once again played two nights at the Rainbow Theatre, on the 23rd and 24th December 1972. What were the audience asked to bring along with them, to the Christmas Eve show?

373. On which TV chat show did David appear in January 1973, along with Elton John, Georgie Fame and Alan Price?

374. Who had designed David's outfit, especially for the show?

375. Which two songs did David perform on the show?

376. What did David give to his host at the end of the recording?

377. Which old school friend did David invite to become his travel companion when setting sail on the SS Canberra from Southampton to New York in January 1973, for the second tour of the US?

378. Which Iggy Pop album was released in February 1973? Although it's said to have been co-produced by Iggy and David, Iggy is at pains to point out that David only 'mixed' the album !

the 1970s

379. Following concerts in the US, to which country did David travel, to perform shows throughout April 1973?
380. During this segment of the 'Ziggy Stardust' tour, which native fashion designer presented David with various costumes for his stage act?

381. What were the B sides to these three singles, all of which charted when released during 1973, each on the RCA record label?
    a) *Drive In Saturday (April)*
    b) *Life On Mars? (June)*
    c) *Sorrow (October)*

382. Name David's 6th studio album, released in April 1973, on the RCA record label.
383. Which make-up artist painted the iconic red and blue lightning bolt across David's face for the album cover shot?
384. In which track did the Reverend Alabaster appear?
385. Which New York Dolls band member was referenced in the track, *Time*?
386. What is the connection between the track, *Lady Grinning Soul* and The Rolling Stones track, *Brown Sugar*?
387. On which track did Marc Bolan play guitar?
388. In the album cover photo taken by Brian Duffy, were David's eyes open or closed?
389. Solve the following anagrams to identify the two album tracks:-
    a) *Intrepid Action*
    b) *Snoring Languidly*

ALL MY ~~IDIOT~~ 1500 QUESTIONS

390. As well as David, which two saxophonists played on the album?
391. Which track was missing its first line of lyric on the inner sleeve lyric sheet?
392. In which track were both Twiggy and Jagger namechecked?

393. In which African State were both the **Aladdin Sane** album and *The Jean Genie* single, banned?

394. At which London venue, in May 1973, did David 'infamously' start the final leg of the 'Ziggy Stardust' tour (aka the 'Aladdin Sane' tour)? The large venue was being used for the first time for a gig of this magnitude, and the sound system simply wasn't adequate. The sound was poor, the audience couldn't hear, and mayhem subsequently ensued.

395. In which magazine, in May 1973, did a weekly column entitled 'My World' appear, supposedly a weekly diary by David of what he was doing?
396. At the time, it was thought that David was actually writing the diaries himself, but that task had been handed to David's new PR, and ex 'Pork' actress who admitted more than forty years later that a lot of it was simply made up ! What is her name?

397. Who answered a 'Girl Friday needed for busy office' ad to work for Mainman in 1973? She became David's personal assistant shortly after, and ultimately began a close personal and working relationship that would last for the rest of his life.

398. Taken from a *Bewlay Brothers* lyric, which English rock band released an album in June 1973, on the Polydor record label, entitled **Kings Of Oblivion**?

399. The famous farewell 'Ziggy Stardust' gig from the Hammersmith Odeon in London took place on the 3rd July 1973. Who filmed the final concert?

400. Like many of the Ziggy shows before it, which piece of music was played through the sound system before David arrived on stage?

401. Which of Mick Ronson's idols made a guest appearance at the concert performing *The Jean Genie/Love Me Do* and *Round and Round* with David and the band?

402. David performed a stunning acoustic version of *My Death* at the gig. Who wrote the song, originally titled *La Mort?*

403. David opened the show with *Hang On To Yourself, Ziggy Stardust* and *Watch That Man* before performing a medley which consisted of which three tracks?

404. Following the "It's the last show we'll ever do" speech, to whom did David turn and point, giving the signal to start the guitar intro for the very last song, *Rock 'N' Roll Suicide?*

405. Who had been the sound engineer for the tour and recorded every show, albeit on one tape that was overwritten each night? As such, the final show recording still exists in full, complete with Garson's piano introduction and Jeff Beck's appearance in the encore.

406. The after show 'retirement' party was attended by many celebrities. Where was it held?

407. At which studios in Pontoise, just outside Paris, did David record his next album, in July 1973? It was to be a collection of some of his favourite songs from the 1960s.

408. Which member of the Spiders from Mars did not go to Paris and did not feature on the new album?

409. Who had replaced him for the project?

410. Which single did Decca re-issue in September 1973, trying to cash in on David's recent success?

411. David was planning a musical based around George Orwell's book, 1984, but the project never came to fruition. Why not?

412. Recorded in October 1973, and broadcast a month later in the US, David performed one last time in 'Ziggy' regalia, for which American TV show?

413. What name was given to David's show?

414. Where in London did filming for the show take place over three days?

415. Who designed many of David's costumes, having previously designed for him in the late1960s for his work with Lindsay Kemp?

416. Who, wearing a nun's habit, sang a duet with David, and which song did they perform?

417. David wore a Freddie Buretti designed white suit for the performance of *Sorrow* featuring which French singer/songwriter? She had herself been the subject

the 1970s

of Roxy Music's **For Your Pleasure** album cover, released earlier in the year.

418. Name David's 7th studio album, released in October 1973, on the RCA record label.
419. *Sorrow* was originally recorded by US band The McCoys in 1965, but which UK act enjoyed a hit with it when released as a single in 1966?
420. The lyrics for only one song were issued with the album. Which song?
421. Which Australian rock band had the original success with F*riday On My Mind*?
422. Which track had originally been recorded by Pink Floyd?
423. Who appeared on the album cover alongside David, and who took the photo?
424. Which track, originally by The Pretty Things, opened the album?
425. Who produced the album?
426. Solve the following anagrams to identify the two album tracks:-
    a) *Cheering Hot Themes*
    b) *Faith's Shep Song*
427. Which two songs by The Who were covered on the album?
428. What instrument was David holding in one of the rear cover photographs taken by Mick Rock?

429. Which two of David's songs were released as A side and B side of a single by Lulu, in January 1974, on the Polydor record label? They had been recorded at

ALL MY ~~IDIOT~~ 1500 QUESTIONS

the Chateau D'Herouvile during the Pin Ups sessions a few months earlier.

430. To which song was David miming when he appeared wearing a black eye patch on the Dutch TV show 'Top Pop', in February 1974?
431. With which award was David presented by the show's host, Ad Visser?

432. Rearrange the following four 1974 singles into chronological order of release.
    a) *Diamond Dogs*
    b) *Knock On Wood*
    c) *Rebel Rebel*
    d) *Rock 'N' Roll Suicide*

433. Mick Ronson's debut solo album, **Slaughter on 10th Avenue**, was released in February 1974, on the RCA record label. For which track on the album did David receive sole writing credit?
434. For which other track, an Italian track written by Lucio Battisti, did David write English lyrics?

435. David contributed saxophone to a track called *To Know Him Is To Love Him* on the album **Now We Are Six**. Released in March 1974, name the artist.

436. Which Dana Gillespie album, co-produced by David and Mick Ronson and featuring songs written by David, was released in March 1974, on the RCA record label?

the 1970s

437. Name David's 8th studio album, released in May 1974, on the RCA record label.
438. Name the instrumental piece of music from the 1940 Richard Rodgers musical 'Pal Joey', that accompanied David's narration in the opening track, *Future Legend*.
439. With which record producer did David renew his association for the album?
440. The cover artwork originated from a photoshoot session with which British photographer?
441. Solve the following anagrams to identify the two album tracks:-
    a) *Net Weights*
    b) *Hero R.T.Gibb*
442. David played many instruments himself on the album but who was brought in to play bass guitar?
443. Who, along with David, co-wrote the track *Rock 'N' Roll With Me?*
444. Which chant closed the album?
445. Which Belgian artist designed the cover artwork?
446. Which track namechecked both Charles Manson and Muhammad Ali?
447. Which two drummers also played on the album?

448. The first leg of the 'Diamond Dogs' tour of North America opened in June 1974, in which Canadian city?
449. Who was the Music Director as well as keyboard player on the first leg of the tour?
450. Who designed the 'Hunger City' theatrical set consisting of skyscrapers, a bridge and a giant hand?

ALL MY ~~IDIOT~~ 1500 QUESTIONS

451. Why was the show in Tampa, Florida on the 2nd July 1974, performed without any of the stage props?
452. Who choreographed the 'Diamond Dogs' shows?
453. Who became David's lead guitar player for the tour, effectively taking over from Mick Ronson?

454. Following a six week break, the second leg of the tour opened in September 1974, in which US city?
455. By what new name did the remainder of the tour become known, following the revised setlist which now included soul songs which David had been writing?
456. Which rhythm guitarist joined this leg of the tour, and in doing so, began a long and successful association with David?
457. Greg Errico replaced Tony Newman on drums for the first two weeks of the second leg of the tour. Which drummer then replaced Greg through to the end of the tour?

458. In September 1974, who met David and ultimately offered him a part in her next film, 'The Blue Bird'? David subsequently declined the offer.

459. Name David's 1st live album, released in October 1974, on the RCA record label?
460. The live album was culled from performances on consecutive nights, at which venue?
461. Which band member led the revolt about money when they learned that the shows were to be recorded for a live album release? The shows were nearly cancelled.

the 1970s

462. Who were the two backing singers/dancers for the shows?

463. In October 1974, Barbara Streisand released an album on the Columbia record label, entitled **Butterfly**. Which of David's songs did she cover on the album?

464. Recorded in November 1974, and broadcast in the US a month later, David appeared on 'The Dick Cavett Show'. As well as giving an infamously 'high on substance' interview, David performed which three songs?

465. What was the title of the Omnibus documentary that was broadcast by the BBC in January 1975, having been filmed for the most part during the US tour of 1974?

466. Who appeared in the documentary as David's driver? He had also been hired as another bodyguard.

467. The documentary showed David using a 'cut up' technique for producing song lyrics. This technique already had a rich history but who had used it in his work throughout the late 1950s and early 1960s, inspiring David to experiment in this way?

468. Who at the BBC, directed, produced and narrated the film?

469. The relationship between David and Defries had soured by 1975. Who was the lawyer who, in February 1975, helped David out of his association with Defries?

470. Listed here are the B sides to the three singles that all charted during 1975, when released on the RCA record label. What were the A sides?
    a) *Suffragette City* (February)
    b) *Right* (July)
    c) *Can You Hear Me?* (November)

471. To whom did David present the award for the 'Best Female Soul Singer' at the 17th annual 'Grammy Awards' in New York, in March 1975?

472. Name David's 9th studio album, released in March 1975, on the RCA record label.

473. Which studio in Philadelphia was one of three studios used for recording the album, the other two being in New York?

474. Which unknown backing singer on the album received a co-writing credit on one of the tracks? His own composition *Funky Music*, had been the template for what became *Fascination*.

475. Solve the following anagrams to identify the two album tracks:-
    a) *House Transceivers*
    b) *Honey Marceau*

476. Which Beatle contributed to the album?

477. Which Sly and the Family Stone member played drums on the album?

478. Which track, when released as a single in the US, gave David his first No. 1 in the US Billboard Hot 100 Chart?

479. Which married couple appeared on the album?

the 1970s

480. Other than Tony Visconti, which other American record producer was involved in producing the album?
481. Which track closed Side One of the vinyl album and featured friend, Geoff MacCormack, on backing vocals?
482. Which track was a heavily reworked version of *I Am Divine*, originally recorded during The Astronettes sessions of 1973?

483. Name the compilation double album which when released by Deram in May 1975, featured an up-to-date soul photo of David on the front cover. The album had originally been released in 1973 in the US, where it featured a cartoon cover depicting characters or situations from each song.

484. In May 1975, which track from the **Hunky Dory** album was released as a single by the British cappella vocal ensemble, The King's Singers?

485. By the mid-1970s, Angie Bowie was planning her own career as a model. By what name was she trying to get herself known?

486. The song *Space Oddity* was re-released in September 1975 by RCA but with a different B side to the original 1969 release. The new release had a two-track B side and it gave David his first No. 1 single in the UK. Which two tracks were on the B side?

ALL MY ~~IDIOT~~ 1500 QUESTIONS

487. On which predominantly African-American Soul music show, did David appear in November 1975, becoming one of only a few white acts to do so?
488. To which two songs did David mime on the show?

489. With whom did David perform a medley of songs starting and finishing with *Young Americans*, on her American TV show, broadcast in the US in November 1975?
490. As well as also performing *Fame* on the show, David and his host performed a duet of which other of David's songs?

491. David appeared on the 'Russell Harty Show' for a second time, in November 1975. The interview was in parts somewhat awkward and conducted via a satellite link. Harty was in London, where was David?
492. The interview ended by showing the 'Soul Train' video clip of David performing *Golden Years* but by what name did Harty mistakenly introduce the track?

493. Name David's 10th studio album, released in January 1976, on the RCA record label.
494. Previously recorded by both Johnny Mathis and Nina Simone, which track was not written by David?
495. Other than the title track, which other track name starts with the letter 'S'?
496. Who was recruited to play bass guitar?
497. Which track opened Side Two of the vinyl album?
498. In what capacity was Steve Shapiro involved with the album?

the 1970s

499. Solve the following anagrams to identify the two album tracks:-
   a) *Anton Is Tattooist*
   b) *Rowan Godwin*
500. Who played piano on the album?
501. At which studios in Los Angeles was the album predominantly recorded?
502. Which track did David claim was offered to, but turned down by, Elvis Presley?
503. Who, along with David, co-produced the album?

504. Known as 'The Station To Station' Tour, 'The Thin White Duke' Tour, 'The Isolar' Tour or 'The White Light' Tour, in which North American city, in February 1976, did David's next Worldwide Concert Tour begin?
505. Impeccably dressed in a white shirt with black waistcoat and black trousers, what was the name of David's new persona or character, associated with the new album and the tour?
506. Which 1929 Salvador Dali film was shown at the beginning of each concert?
507. Who or what was 'Raw Moon'?
508. Who played lead guitar on the tour?
509. Which three band members became David's rhythm section for the rest of the decade and were collectively and affectionately known as the DAM trio?
510. When David returned to the UK in May 1976 to continue the world tour, a photo emerged of David appearing to give a Nazi salute, thereby causing great controversy. David's explanation was that he had been waving to the waiting crowds and the camera

just happened to catch him mid wave. At which London train station did the incident occur?

511. In which New York State city was David arrested for possession of marijuana, in March 1976? Charges were subsequently dropped.

512. In what context were milk, cocaine and red peppers significant to the David Bowie story?

513. Broadcast on American TV in March 1976, on whose show did David perform *Stay* and *Five Years*, as well as being interviewed by the host?
514. In what capacity did Dwain Vaughns also appear on the show?

515. Released in March 1976, which film gave David his first major acting role?
516. Who had cast David and also directed the film?
517. What was the name of David's alien character?
518. In a scene from the film in which co-star Rip Torn entered a record shop, which of David's album covers could be seen hanging on the wall?
519. Who played the part of David's leading lady, Mary-Lou?
520. Who did the artwork for a reprint of the book by Walter Tevis on which the film was based?
521. Which award, presented by the 'Academy of Science Fiction, Fantasy and Horror Films', did David win for 'Best Actor'?

the 1970s

522. Only one single release charted during 1976 (April). With *We Are The Dead* on the B side, what was the A side?
523. The vocal intro of the single was essentially lifted from which Yardbirds song, released back in 1964?

524. Released in May 1976 on the RCA record label, what was the title of the first real meaningful compilation album of David's hits from 1969 to 1976?
525. The first 1000 copies pressed in the UK, contained a different version of one track, to all those copies pressed later. Which track?
526. Interestingly, two tracks on the compilation had never been released as singles. Name the tracks, both of which were taken from **The Rise and Fall of Ziggy Stardust and the Spiders from Mars** album.

527. By the end of 1976, David had left Los Angeles and lived for a time in Switzerland, before finally settling in which European city?
528. Living in a modest flat above a car spares shop, what was David's new address?
529. Who had David taken with him, in the hope that they could both kick the drugs habit together?

530. Name David's 11th studio album, released in January 1977, on the RCA record label.
531. What had been the original working title for the album?
532. Which 1970 UK Eurovision Song Contest entrant, sang the intro on the track, *Sound And Vision*?

533. Solve the following anagrams to identify the two album tracks:-
    a) *American Glassware Hyacinths*
    b) *Withhold New Art*
534. Which two European studios were used to record the album?
535. Which member of glam rock band Roxy Music, worked on this and the next two studio albums with David? He also received a co-writing credit for *Warszawa*.
536. At less than two minutes, which track on the album was the shortest in length?
537. The Oblique Strategy cards used on the album to promote creativity were originally designed and produced in 1975 by Brian Eno and which multimedia artist?
538. Name the four instrumental tracks that made up Side Two of the vinyl album.
539. Who, at Tony Visconti's suggestion, played guitar on the album having previously worked on Visconti's album, **Inventory**?
540. Using a still from 'The Man Who Fell To Earth' film, who designed the cover artwork?

541. *Sound And Vision* was released as a single, in February 1977, on the RCA record label. Which instrumental was on the B side?

542. Who did hairdresser Suzi Fussey marry, in March 1977?

the 1970s

543. In what capacity was David involved with the Iggy Pop tour that started at Aylesbury Friars, in March 1977?

544. Which Iggy Pop album, released in March 1977 on the RCA record label, did David produce?

545. Tracks on the album were co-written by David and Iggy but which track was also co-written by Carlos Alomar?

546. Which track from the **Low** album failed to reach the Top 40 in the UK when released as a single in June 1977, on the RCA record label? *Speed Of Life* was its B side.

547. On whose TV show did David appear, in September 1977, just a week or so before the host's tragic death in a car accident? The show was broadcast later that month.

548. Which song from his upcoming new album did David perform on the show?

549. Which song were David and Marc performing together at the end of the show, when Marc fell from the stage?

550. Which band was also booked to appear on the show but never did due to time restrictions?

551. Recorded in September 1977 and broadcast on Christmas Eve the same year, on whose 'Merrie Olde Christmas' TV show did David appear performing *Heroes?*

ALL MY ~~IDIOT~~ 1500 QUESTIONS

552. What was the title of the Christmas duet David sang with his host?

553. The *Heroes* single was released in September 1977 on the RCA record label. In which two other languages was the song recorded by David and what were their titles?

554. Name David's 12th studio album, released in October 1977, on the RCA record label.

555. What slogan was used by RCA to market the new album? It began 'There's old wave, ... '.

556. The album included a lyric sheet for the first time since which earlier album?

557. Which song was in part a tribute to American artist Chris Burden who was famous for having himself crucified to a Volkswagen Beetle car in 1974?

558. To whom was the track *V-2 Schneider* a tribute?

559. The album cover was inspired by a 1917 painting, 'Roquairol', by which German artist?

560. Which German experimental musician had originally been lined up to play on the album, before ultimately being replaced by Robert Fripp?

561. Solve the following anagrams to identify the two album tracks:-
    a) *Stefan Holstein's Ego*
    b) *Haunted State Abbey*

562. Which track was co-written by Carlos Alomar?

563. Which backing singer on the album was spotted kissing Tony Visconti by the wall, giving David lyric ideas for the title track?

the 1970s

564. Which track was named after the district in Berlin whose population is made up largely of Turkish immigrants?

565. David appeared on the Dutch TV show 'TopPop' in October 1977 and was presented with two gold discs for which two albums?

566. Released in January 1978 on the RCA record label, which track became David's only Top 40 single of the whole year? The instrumental track *Sense Of Doubt* was on the B side.

567. The 'Isolar II' or 'Stage' or 'The Low/Heroes' Worldwide Concert Tour kicked off in March 1978, in which Californian city?

568. Who played keyboards on the tour, keeping a diary which in 1999 he turned into a book called 'We Can Be Heroes – Life On Tour with David Bowie'?

569. Adrian Belew joined David's band for the world tour. For whom had Adrian been working when offered the gig by David?

570. The UK leg of the world tour started in June 1978, in which English city?

571. David took his world tour to Australia for the first time, in November 1978. In which South Australian city was the first concert held?

572. Who was Dennis Garcia?

573. Released in May 1978 on green vinyl, which 1936 classical composition by Prokofiev did David narrate?

574. David was third choice to narrate the story, behind Alec Guinness and which other British actor, both of whom turned down the offer?
575. The music itself was played by the Philadelphia Orchestra, but which Hungarian born American violinist conducted the orchestra?

576. In May 1978, David and the band travelled to the Beat Club studios in Bremen to record a session for which German TV programme? The show was later broadcast in August 1978.

577. Name David's 2nd live album, released in September 1978, on the RCA record label.
578. On what colour vinyl were initial copies of the album pressed?
579. *Sense Of Doubt* from the **"Heroes"** album appeared on Side Three of the double vinyl album but which three instrumental tracks from the **Low** album also appeared on Side Three?
580. Which five tracks from **The Rise and Fall of Ziggy Stardust and the Spiders from Mars** album, took up the whole of Side One?

581. First released in West Germany, in November 1978, what was the name of the film in which David appeared?
582. Who was Paul Von Pryzgodski?
583. Who directed the film?
584. Which of these actors was NOT in the film:-
    a) Marlene Dietrich
    b) Sydne Rome

the 1970s

      c) Susan Sarandon
      d) Kim Novak

585. Which song did David co-write (with Jack Fishman) for the soundtrack album?

586. 1979 saw three charting single releases on the RCA record label. Listed here in alphabetical order, place the singles in chronological order of release.
      a) *Boys Keep Swinging*
      b) *DJ*
      c) *John I'm Only Dancing (Again)*

587. Broadcast in April 1979, on which British comedian's video show did David appear?

588. Which song did David perform on the show?

589. Following Lou Reed's Hammersmith Odeon show in April 1979, at which Knightsbridge restaurant did David and Lou famously come to blows?

590. What was the title of the BBC Radio One show, broadcast in May 1979, in which David played DJ for two hours, playing tracks from some of his favourite artists?

591. Name David's 13th studio album, released in May 1979, on the RCA record label.

592. Which track contained a section of *All The Young Dudes*, played backwards?

593. Inspired by Eno's Oblique Strategies Cards, on which track did Carlos Alomar play drums and Dennis Davis play bass guitar?

594. Solve the following anagrams to identify the two album tracks:-
    a) *High Inflating Craft*
    b) *Nickola Karo BEng*
595. What address can be seen on the postcard on the album cover?
596. Which song had the same tune as a song on Iggy Pop's **The Idiot** album, but with a different title and different lyrics?
597. What colour was Anne's silk blouse?
598. It was known as the third album in the Berlin Trilogy, but in which studios was the album predominantly recorded?
599. Which two tracks on the album share the same chord progression?
600. With which English artist did David collaborate on the cover artwork and design?
601. Who played violin on the album?

602. Broadcast in December 1979, on which NBC TV show did David appear, with the inimitable Klaus Nomi in tow?
603. Which three songs did he perform?

604. On whose 1979 New Year's Eve show did David appear, performing a newly arranged acoustic version of *Space Oddity*?
605. Which musician (and David Bowie fan) was also booked to be on the show but had to be escorted away when David objected to his presence?

the 1970s
373 Answers

233. *Harlequin* and *Columbine*
234. *Threepenny Pierrot*
235. *When I Live My Dream*
236. Pierrot In Turquoise Or The Looking Glass Murders
237. Mick Ronson
238. The Sunday Show
239. Hype
240. John Cambridge, Mick Ronson and Tony Visconti
241. Liz Hartley
242. a) John was Cowboyman
    b) Mick was Gangsterman
    c) Tony was Hypeman
    d) David was Rainbowman
243. *The Prettiest Star*
244. Marc Bolan
245. Decca
246. 20th March 1970
247. Bromley Registry Office

248. Clare Shenstone and John Cambridge
249. David's mum Peggy replaced John Cambridge
250. Peruvian bangles
251. The Tony Visconti Trio
252. Mick 'Woody' Woodmansey
253. Tony Defries
254. Olav Wyper
255. Laurence Myers
256. GEM Music Group
257. Ivor Novello Award for the most original song
258. *Memory of a Free Festival (Parts 1 & 2)*
259. Bob Grace
260. *Holy Holy / Black Country Rock*
261. USA
262. Ron Oberman
263. Doug Yule
264. Freddie Buretti
265. Rudi Valentino
266. *Moonage Daydream, Hang On To Yourself, Looking For A Friend* and *Man In The Middle*
267. *Rupert The Riley*
268. *Miss Peculiar*
269. *The Width Of A Circle*
270. **The Man Who Sold The World**
271. Jimmy Page
272. a) *All The Madmen*
    b) *She Shook Me Cold*
273. Ralph Mace
274. Mr. Fish Boutique
275. Mike Weller
276. *After All (oh by jingo)*
277. Metrobolist

the 1970s

278. Tony Visconti
279. *The Width Of A Circle, The Man Who Sold The World* and *The Supermen*
280. Khalil Gibran
281. Peter Noone
282. David Bowie
283. Minnie Bell Music Ltd
284. Trevor Bolder
285. 30 May 1971
286. Duncan Zowie Haywood Jones
287. *Kooks*
288. In Concert
289. George Underwood
290. Dana Gillespie
291. Glastonbury
292. Mick Ronson
293. Dudley Moore
294. Dana Gillespie
295. Dennis Katz
296. Pork
297. The Country Club
298. Amanda Pork (based on Brigid Berlin)
299. Cherry Vanilla
300. False, Andy loathed it, although he did like David's yellow shoes
301. Mick Ronson
302. *Right On Mother*
303. Christopher Lee
304. Mary Hopkin
305. **Hunky Dory**
306. a) *The Bewlay Brothers*
    b) *Song For Bob Dylan*

307. Ken Scott (assisted by the actor)
308. *Kooks*
309. *Life On Mars?*
310. *Fill Your Heart*
311. George Underwood and Terry Pastor
312. Rick Wakeman
313. *Eight Line Poem*
314. The regular rear cover was also the front cover for the New Zealand release.
315. *Queen Bitch*
316. Tony Blackburn
317. The Legendary Stardust Cowboy
318. Suzi Fussey
319. John Peel
320. Bob Harris
321. *Queen Bitch*
322. Michael Watts
323. Melody Maker
324. Aylesbury Friars
325. Roger Taylor and Freddie Mercury
326. The Old Grey Whistle Test (Bob Harris took over from Richard for Series Two and is the name most synonymous with the show. *Oh You Pretty Things* was not broadcast until much later).
327. Toby Jug, Tolworth
328. Nicky Graham
329. *Starman*
330. Olga Archbold
331. The Spiders from Mars
332. b) *Starman (April 1972)*
    a) *John I'm Only Dancing (September 1972)*
    c) *The Jean Genie (November 1972)*

the 1970s

333. *The Supermen*
334. Johnnie Walker Lunchtime Show
335. **The Rise and Fall of Ziggy Stardust and the Spiders from Mars**
336. To be played at maximum volume
337. Heddon Street
338. Mark Carr Pritchard's guitar
339. a) *Hang On To Yourself*
    b) *Suffragette City*
340. Ron Davies
341. A Clockwork Orange
342. Marc Bolan
343. *Tony (Star)*
344. Dana Gillespie (She was credited on later re-issues).
345. *Rock 'N' Roll Suicide*
346. Lift Off with Ayshea
347. Mick Rock
348. Oxford Town Hall
349. Melody Maker
350. Alice Cooper
351. Mainman
352. Robin Lumley
353. Save The Whale benefit for Friends of the Earth
354. Kenny Everett
355. *I'm Waiting For The Man*
356. *All The Young Dudes* (they had already turned down *Suffragette City* and following the success of *Dudes*, they would go on to turn down *Drive In Saturday*)
357. **Transformer**
358. Ronnie Ross
359. The Rainbow Theatre
360. Lindsay Kemp

ALL MY ~~IDIOT~~ 1500 QUESTIONS

361. Roxy Music
362. George Underwood
363. Manchester
364. QE2 from Southampton to New York
365. Mike Garson
366. Stuey George and Tony Frost
367. Cleveland
368. Santa Monica
369. Drive In Saturday
370. The **David Bowie** Philips album had been re-titled **Space Oddity**
371. Don't Sit Down
372. A toy for children in care and in hospitals. All toys were subsequently delivered to Dr. Barnado's homes in London
373. Russell Harty Plus Pop
374. Freddie Buretti
375. Drive In Saturday and *My Death*
376. The single chandelier earring he had been wearing
377. Geoff MacCormack
378. Raw Power
379. Japan
380. Kansai Yamamoto
381. a) Round And Round
   b) The Man Who Sold The World
   c) Amsterdam
382. **Aladdin Sane** (his first UK No.1 album)
383. Pierre LaRoche
384. Watch That Man
385. Billy Murcia (*billy dolls*)
386. Both are said to have been inspired by American soul singer Claudia Lennear

387. Marc didn't play on the album, he only played guitar on the single version of *The Prettiest Star*. The album version was played by Ronson.
388. Closed
389. a) *Panic In Detroit*
b) *Lady Grinning Soul*
390. Ken Fordham and Brian 'Bux' Wilshaw
391. Cracked Actor
392. Drive In Saturday
393. Rhodesia (now Zimbabwe)
394. Earls Court
395. Mirabelle Magazine
396. Cherry Vanilla
397. Corinne Schwab (Coco)
398. Pink Fairies
399. D. A. Pennebaker
400. *Ode To Joy* from Beethoven's 9th Symphony
401. Jeff Beck
402. Jacques Brel
403. Wild Eyed Boy From Freecloud, All The Young Dudes and *Oh You Pretty Things*
404. John 'Hutch' Hutchinson
405. Robin Mayhew
406. Café Royal in Regent Street
407. Chateau D'Herouville Studios
408. Mick 'Woody' Woodmansey
409. Aynsley Dunbar
410. The Laughing Gnome / The Gospel According To Tony Day
411. Orwell's wife Sonia, would not grant permission for her late husband's work to be used
412. The Midnight Special

413. The 1980 Floor Show
414. The Marquee, Soho
415. Natasha Kornilof
416. Marianne Faithful. They sang Sonny & Cher's, *I Got You Babe*
417. Amanda Lear
418. **Pin Ups**
419. The Merseys
420. Where Have All The Good Times Gone
421. The Easybeats
422. See Emily Play
423. Twiggy, taken during a photoshoot in Paris, for Vogue magazine, by her then partner, Justin de Villeneuve
424. Rosalyn
425. Ken Scott
426. a) *Here Comes The Night*
   b) *Shapes Of Things*
427. *I Can't Explain* and *Anyway Anyhow Anywhere*
428. Saxophone
429. The Man Who Sold The World / Watch That Man
430. Rebel Rebel
431. The Edison Award for the Most Popular Male Vocalist
432. c) *Rebel Rebel (February)*
   d) *Rock 'N' Roll Suicide (April)*
   a) *Diamond Dogs (June)*
   b) *Knock On Wood (September)*
433. Growing Up And I'm Fine
434. Music Is Lethal
435. Steeleye Span
436. **Weren't Born A man**
437. **Diamond Dogs**
438. Bewitched, Bothered and Bewildered

439. Tony Visconti
440. Terry O'Neill
441. a) *Sweet Thing*
     b) *Big Brother*
442. Herbie Flowers
443. Warren Peace (Geoff MacCormack)
444. *Chant Of The Ever Circling Skeletal Family*
445. Guy Peellaert
446. *Candidate (Charlie Manson, Cassius Clay)*
447. Tony Newman and Aynsley Dunbar
448. Montreal
449. Michael Kamen
450. Jules Fisher and Mark Ravitz
451. The truck driver carrying the set had been stung by a bee and ended up in a ditch
452. Toni Basil
453. Earl Slick
454. Los Angeles
455. The Philly Dogs Tour
456. Carlos Alomar
457. Dennis Davis
458. Elizabeth Taylor
459. David Live
460. The Tower Theatre, Philadelphia
461. Herbie Flowers
462. Warren Peace and Gui Andrisano
463. *Life On Mars?*
464. *1984, Young Americans* and *Footstompin'*
465. Cracked Actor
466. Tony Mascia
467. William Burroughs
468. Alan Yentob

469. Michael Lippman
470. a) *Young Americans*
    b) *Fame*
    c) *Golden Years*
471. Aretha Franklyn
472. Young Americans
473. Sigma Sound Studios
474. Luther Vandross
475. a) *Across The Universe*
    b) *Can You Hear Me?*
476. John Lennon
477. Andy Newmark
478. *Fame*
479. Carlos Alomar and Robin Clark
480. Harry Maslin
481. *Right*
482. *Somebody Up There Likes Me*
483. Images 1966 - 1967
484. *Life On Mars?*
485. Jipp Jones
486. *Changes* and *Velvet Goldmine*
487. Soul Train (after Elton John and The Average White Band)
488. *Fame* and *Golden Years*
489. Cher
490. *Can You Hear Me?*
491. Burbank, Los Angeles
492. *Golden Tears*
493. Station To Station
494. *Wild Is The Wind*
495. *Stay*
496. George Murray

the 1970s

497. *TVC15*
498. Steve designed the cover artwork
499. a) *Station To Station*
     b) *Word On A Wing*
500. Roy Bittan
501. Cherokee Studios
502. *Golden Years*
503. Harry Maslin
504. Vancouver, Canada
505. The Thin White Duke
506. Un Chien Andalou
507. The touring band collectively became known as Raw Moon
508. Stacey Heydon
509. Dennis **D**avis, Carlos **A**lomar and George **M**urray
510. Victoria Station
511. Rochester
512. David himself has said this is basically all he was living on during the drug fuelled years of the mid-1970s
513. The Dinah Shore Show
514. Dwain was a Karate black belt and friend of David's; they acted out a self-defence demonstration.
515. The Man Who Fell To Earth
516. Nicholas Roeg
517. Thomas Jerome Newton
518. **Young Americans**
519. Candy Clark
520. George Underwood
521. A Saturn Award
522. *TVC15*
523. *Good Morning Little Schoolgirl*

ALL MY ~~IDIOT~~ 1500 QUESTIONS

524. **Changesonebowie**
525. *John I'm Only Dancing* (the sax version was on the first 1000 copies pressed)
526. *Ziggy Stardust* and *Suffragette City*, the latter of which would be released as a single, two months later, in support of the compilation album.
527. Berlin
528. 155 Hauptstrasse, Schoeneburg, Berlin
529. Iggy Pop
530. **Low**
531. New Music: Night And Day
532. Mary Hopkin
533. a) *Always Crashing In The Same Car*
     b) *What In The World*
534. Chateau D'Herouville studios near Paris and Hansa By The Wall studios in Berlin
535. Brian Eno
536. *Breaking Glass*
537. Peter Schmidt
538. *Warszawa, Art Decade, Weeping Wall* and *Subterraneans*
539. Ricky Gardiner
540. George Underwood
541. *A New Career In A New Town*
542. Mick Ronson
543. David played keyboards on the tour
544. **The Idiot**
545. *Sister Midnight*
546. *Be My Wife*
547. Marc Bolan's 'Marc' show
548. *Heroes*
549. *Standing Next To You*

550. Eddie And The Hotrods
551. Bing Crosby's show
552. *Peace On Earth/Little Drummer Boy*
553. *Helden* in German and *Heros* in French
554. **"Heroes"**
555. "There's old wave, there's new wave, and there's David Bowie"
556. **Aladdin Sane**
557. *Joe The Lion*
558. Kraftwerk's Florian Schneider
559. Erich Heckel
560. Michael Rother
561. a) *Sons Of The Silent Age*
    b) *Beauty And The Beast*
562. *The Secret Life Of Arabia*
563. Antonia Maass
564. *Neuköln*
565. **Low and "Heroes"**
566. *Beauty And The Beast*
567. San Diego
568. Sean Mayes
569. Frank Zappa
570. Newcastle
571. Adelaide
572. Dennis was the local musician who replaced Roger Powell for the Perth gigs
573. **Peter And The Wolf**
574. Peter Ustinov
575. Eugene Ormandy
576. Musikladen
577. **Stage**
578. Yellow

ALL MY ~~IDIOT~~ 1500 QUESTIONS

579. *Warszawa, Speed Of Life* and *Art Decade*
580. *Hang On To Yourself, Ziggy Stardust, Five Years, Soul Love* and *Star*
581. Just A Gigolo
582. A Prussian Officer, and the character played by David
583. David Hemmings
584. c) Susan Sarandon wasn't
585. *Revolutionary Song* performed by The Rebels
586. a) *Boys Keep Swinging* (April)
     b) *DJ* (June)
     c) *John I'm Only Dancing (Again)* (December)
587. Kenny Everett
588. *Boys Keep Swinging*
589. The Chelsea Rendezvous
590. Star Special
591. **Lodger**
592. *Move On*
593. *Boys Keep Swinging*
594. a) *African Night Flight*
     b) *Look Back In Anger*
595. David Bowie, c/o RCA Records, 1 Bedford Avenue, London WC1
596. *Red Money* (on **Lodger**), *Sister Midnight* (on **The Idiot**)
597. *Blue (Repetition)*
598. Mountain Studios (Montreux, Switzerland)
599. *Fantastic Voyage* and *Boys Keep Swinging*
600. Derek Boshier
601. Simon House
602. Saturday Night Live
603. *The Man Who Sold The World, TVC15* and *Boys Keep Swinging*

the 1970s

604. Kenny Everett's show
605. Gary Numan

Figure 9: Selection of items from Author's Collection, featuring works from, and recollections of, the 1970s

ALL MY ~~IDIOT~~ 1500 QUESTIONS

the 1980s

Figure 10: Alamy Stock Photo

the 1980s
233 Questions

606. Iggy Pop's **Soldier** album was released in February 1980, on the Arista record label. Which track did David co-write with Iggy, as well as providing backing vocals?

607. On what date in 1980 did David and Angie divorce?

608. Which Kurt Weill & Bertolt Brecht song was released as a single by David in February 1980, on the RCA record label? The 1979 version of *Space Oddity* was on the B side.

609. The Blondie 12" single *Atomic*, was released in February 1980 on the Chrysalis record label. The B side included Blondie's live version of which of David's songs from the 1970s?

610. In the spring of 1980, David travelled to Japan to record a TV commercial for which Japanese drink?
611. What was the name of the piece of music written by David and used in the commercial?

612. The *Ashes To Ashes* single was released in August 1980, on the RCA record label. Which song was on the B side?
613. The ground-breaking music video accompanying the single was filmed at a beach near to Hastings on the South Coast. Who directed it?
614. Which nightclub host and leader of the new wave band Visage, appeared in the music video?
615. What number did the single reach in the UK Singles Charts?

616. From July 1980, David spent six months in the US, playing the lead role in which Bernard Pomerance stage play?
617. Who directed the play having offered David the role some months earlier?
618. Which character did David play?
619. From whom did David take over the role?
620. Which two US cities hosted the production in July/August before it finally reached The Booth Theatre in New York in September, for a three month run?

621. Name David's 14th studio album, released in September 1980, the last one on the RCA record label.
622. Which was the only track not written by David?
623. On which track did Pete Townshend play guitar?

the 1980s

624. Name the Japanese singer on *Its No Game (No. 1)*.
625. Who designed the Pierrot costume seen on the album cover?
626. Solve the following anagrams to identify the two album tracks:-
   a) *Supt. Archibald Whelk*
   b) *Agent Lewie Field*
627. Working with David for the first time since **Station To Station**, who played piano on the album?
628. From which previously unreleased song from around 1970 did David lift lyrics and melody for both *Its No Game* tracks?
629. Who co-produced the album with David?
630. For which track on the album was 'Jamaica' a working title?
631. What was the title of the track recorded back in 1973 by The Astronettes, which ultimately became *Scream Like A Baby*?

632. Backed by *Scream Like A Baby*, which track became the second single to be taken from the album, when released in October 1980, on the RCA record label?

633. Which famous musician and friend of David's, was murdered outside his Dakota apartment in New York, on the 8th December 1980?

634. Which Greatest Hits compilation album was released by K-Tel, in December 1980, in time for the Christmas market?

ALL MY ~~IDIOT~~ 1500 QUESTIONS

635. The title track from the latest album became the third single, released in January 1981, on the RCA record label. What was on the B side?

636. At the 'British Rock And Pop Awards' ceremony in February 1981, from whom did David receive the award for 'Best Male Singer 1980'?

637. Which rockabilly band, in March 1981, released a cover version of David's *John I'm Only Dancing*?

638. Which track became the fourth single from the latest album when released in March 1981, on the RCA record label? The non-album Japanese single *Crystal Japan* was on the B side.

639. Released in Germany in April 1981, name the film about Christiane Felscherinow in which David made a cameo appearance as himself in concert.
640. Wearing a red jacket, which song did David perform for the film?
641. Which German actress played the lead role in the film?

642. First broadcast in September 1981, which popular BBC TV comedy series contained the following lyrics in its closing theme tune?
   TVs
   Deep freeze
   And David Bowie LPs

643. Name the book written by Angie Bowie about life with David, published in 1981.

the 1980s

644. Name the track released as a single in October 1981, which David had co-written with the band, Queen.
645. At which recording studios in Switzerland was the track recorded?
646. Who came up with the instantly recognisable bassline?
647. The track did not appear on any of David's original studio albums, but on which Queen album did it appear the following year?

648. Previously recorded by both Johnny Matthis and Nina Simone, which Dimitri Tiomkin song did David cover, releasing it as a single in November 1981, on the RCA record label? *Golden Years* was on the B side.

649. What was the title of the second RCA compilation album of hits, released in November 1981, this time presenting tracks from *Oh You Pretty Things* in 1971 to *Ashes To Ashes* in 1980?

650. David released no new studio albums during the whole of 1981. In which year did David last release no new studio albums in the UK?

651. Recorded in late 1981, and broadcast in March 1982 by the BBC, David played the lead role in which Bertolt Brecht play?
652. What was Baal's full name?
653. Who directed the play?
654. A vinyl EP was later released consisting of five songs. *Baal's Hymn* and *Remembering Marie A* were on one side, which three tracks were on the other?

ALL MY ~~IDIOT~~ 1500 QUESTIONS

655. The B side was *Paul's Theme (Jogging Chase)* but what was the A side of David's next single, released in April 1982 on the MCA record label?
656. David had written the lyrics for the single, who wrote the music?
657. The track was taken from the feature film of the same name. Who directed the film and asked David to collaborate on the soundtrack?

658. Which of David's songs from 1972 was released as a single in October 1982, on the Beggars Banquet record label, by the English rock band, Bauhaus?

659. Having been recorded back in 1977, which single was finally released in November 1982, in time for the Christmas market? David's *Fantastic Voyage* was on the B side.

660. In November 1982, RCA released a set of ten 7" picture discs of old hit singles, ranging from *Space Oddity* through to *Ashes To Ashes*. Packaged in a small presentation folder or wallet, what was the name of the set of discs?

661. By the end of 1982, David was living at the Chateau du Signal, a 14-room mansion built in which Swiss city on the shores of Lake Geneva?

662. David began 1983 by signing a new five year recording contract with which record label?

the 1980s

663. At which London hotel did David give a press conference, in March 1983, to announce an upcoming new album for the new record label, and also a world tour?

664. First premiered at the Cannes Film Festival in May 1983, in which supernatural horror film did David appear?
665. Who wrote the novel of the same name, on which the film was based?
666. Which character did David play?
667. Name the two leading lady actresses in the film, one played the character Miriam Blaylock and the other played Sarah Roberts.
668. Who directed the film?

669. Which song, released in March 1983 on the EMI record label, became the lead single from the upcoming new album? A new version of the previously released *Cat People (Putting Out Fire)*, was on the B side.
670. Who directed the accompanying music video for the single?
671. In which New South Wales town was the music video filmed?
672. Name the two main Australian Aborigine students who appeared in the music video.

673. Name David's 15th studio album, released in April 1983, the first one on the EMI record label.
674. Who co-produced the album with David?

675. Which three album track names all start with the letter '*C*'?
676. The album was recorded at the Power Station Studios, in which US city?
677. Which American photographer took the front cover photograph of David shadow boxing?
678. Which instruments did David play on the album?
679. Who played lead guitar on the album?
680. Solve the following anagrams to identify the two album tracks:-
    a) *Lemon Dover*
    b) *Ice Torch*
681. Which track was co-written by David and Iggy Pop?
682. Which English rock band had originally written and recorded *Criminal World* in 1977?
683. Which two drummers played on the album?

684. In support of the new album, David began the new Worldwide Concert Tour in May 1983, in which European capital city?
685. What was the name of the tour?
686. Which band member became Music Director for the tour?
687. Following David throughout the tour, on and off stage, who was appointed official photographer?
688. Stevie Ray Vaughan was the intended lead guitarist for the tour (as he had been on the album) but who replaced him at the last minute?
689. What role did Jim Callaghan play?
690. For which organisation did David perform a special charity concert, in June 1983, at the Hammersmith Odeon in London?

the 1980s

691. In which Canadian city was the 13th July 1983 show recorded for American FM Radio broadcast?
692. At which venue in Vancouver, on 12th September 1983, was the show filmed for a live concert VHS video release the following year?
693. Thrashing Earl Slick's guitar in the process, who joined David on stage in Toronto, in September 1983 for a one off appearance, performing *The Jean Genie*?
694. For a rendition of which song on tour, did David's props include a skull, a cloak and dark sunglasses, a la Hamlet?
695. Who were the two backing singers on the tour?
696. In what way did David pay tribute to his friend John Lennon, on the 8th December in Hong Kong, the very last night of the tour?
697. By the end of the tour, what had been nicknamed 'Bungle In The Jungle' by David's associates?

698. Entered into the 1983 Cannes Film Festival in May 1983, in which film did David star as a New Zealand soldier in a Japanese Prisoner of War camp, in 1942?
699. In which self-governing island country in the South Pacific Ocean, was the film predominantly made?
700. Which Japanese film director and screenwriter directed the film?
701. Which character did David play?
702. Which British actor played the lead role of Mr. Lawrence (Lt. Col. John Lawrence)?
703. Which Japanese musician starred in the film as Capt. Yonoi, as well as writing the soundtrack music?

ALL MY ~~IDIOT~~ 1500 QUESTIONS

704. The single *China Girl / Shake It* was released in May 1983 on the EMI record label. Who was the New Zealand model who featured in the accompanying music video?

705. Which American actor, with a career spanning 60 years, was namechecked in the lyrics of *China Girl*?

706. Released in June 1983, what was the name of the film in which David appeared, alongside Eric Idle (Duncan Jones' Godfather), John Cleese and Graham Chapman, to name but three?

707. David made a brief cameo appearance as which character?

708. The third and final single to be taken from the latest album was released in September 1983, on the EMI record label. With a live version of *Modern Love* on its B side, what was the A side?

709. Which live double album did RCA release in October 1983, some ten years after it had been recorded at the Hammersmith Odeon?

710. By the end of 1983, which of David's early managers had published a book entitled 'The Pitt Report', about life with David in the 1960s?

711. Originally recorded at the start of 1969, which promotional film was finally released on VHS video, by Polygram, in May 1984?

the 1980s

712. Which of David's songs did Tina Turner cover on her **Private Dancer** album, released in May 1984?

713. In which James Bond movie did David turn down the offer to play villain Max Zorin, in mid-1984? The part went to American actor Christopher Walken and the film was released the following year.

714. *Blue Jean* was released as the lead single from the upcoming new album, in September 1984, on the EMI record label. What was the title of the 20 minute extended music video film that accompanied the release of the single?

715. Who directed the extended music video film?

716. Played by David, what was the name of the flamboyant rock star in the music video?

717. What was the name of the character also played by David, who was attempting to win the affections of a beautiful girl by claiming to know the rock star personally?

718. The girl's character in the video was 'The Dream'. Which actress played the role?

719. Name the David Bowie lookalike and stand-in who also appeared in the music video film.

720. Name David's 16th studio album, released in September 1984, on the EMI record label.

721. The album was recorded at Le Studio, Morin-Heights, in which country?

722. Part way through the recording, original producer Derek Bramble had a falling out with David that led

to his departure. Already in the fold as engineer, who took over production duties?

723. Which two tracks on the album were the only two to be written solely by David?
724. Who performed a duet with David on the title track?
725. Solve the following anagrams to identify the two album tracks:-
    a) *Leigh Valentino*
    b) *Trent Wild Album*
726. Which of these musicians did NOT play on the album?
    a) Carlos Alomar (Guitars)
    b) Mike Garson (Keyboards)
    c) Omar Hakim (Drums)
    d) Carmine Rojas (Bass)
727. Co-written by David, Iggy Pop and Carlos Alomar, which track closed the album?
728. As well as covering Iggy Pop's *Don't Look Down* on the album, which two Iggy tracks from his **Lust For Life** album in 1977, did David also cover?
729. Another cover, *God Only Knows*, penned by Brian Wilson and Tony Asher, was originally a hit for which American rock band in 1966?
730. Who designed the cover artwork, having already done the same for the **Let's Dance** album the previous year?

731. In 1984, David recorded an alternative introduction to the Raymond Briggs animation film which was first broadcast on Christmas TV in 1982. Briggs himself had performed the original introduction. What was the film?

the 1980s

732. For which music video did David win the 'Best Male Video' award at the 'MTV Video Music Awards' in September 1984, held at the Radio City Music Hall in New York?
733. Which other award was presented to David at the same awards ceremony?

734. Which track, in November 1984, became the second single to be taken from the **Tonight** album? The B side was *Tumble And Twirl*.

735. Which line of lyric did David sing in the Band Aid charity single *Do They Know It's Christmas*, released in December 1984?

736. After suffering years of mental issues, how in January 1985 did David's half-brother Terry, die?

737. With which American jazz band did David record and release a single on the EMI record label, in February 1985? The B side was an instrumental version of the A side.
738. Name the single.
739. From which film was the single taken?

740. At the 27th annual 'Grammy Awards' held in February 1985 in Los Angeles, which award did David win for his extended music video film, **Jazzin' For Blue Jean**?

ALL MY ~~IDIOT~~ 1500 QUESTIONS

741. First released in the US, in February 1985, what was the title of the film in which David played a small time British Crook?
742. Who directed the film?
743. What was the name of David's character?
744. Who played the lead roles of Ed Okin and Diana respectively?

745. As a special guest at whose Birmingham NEC concert did David make a surprise appearance in March 1985?
746. Which Canadian artist also made a guest appearance at the same show?

747. Released in May 1985, and backed by *Don't Look Down*, name the only solo single released by David that year.
748. Who co-directed the accompanying music video with David?

749. At which Wembley Stadium extravaganza, organized by Bob Geldof and Midge Ure, did David appear in July 1985?
750. Which Royal couple were in attendance?
751. Following a few bars of the national anthem by the Coldstream Guards, which act opened proceedings with a rousing rendition of *Rockin' All Over The World*?
752. Which band performed immediately before David?
753. Which four songs did David perform?
754. Which fifth song had David originally intended to perform, but due to time constraints, opted to introduce *that* video of the Ethiopian famine instead?

the 1980s

755. Which track by The Cars accompanied the famine video?
756. David's backing group for the occasion were put together at short notice. Who played the saxophone?
757. Who played keyboards?
758. With whom did David collaborate to make a music video, especially for the event?
759. Which song did they perform for the music video? It reached No. 1 in the UK charts when released as a single, in August 1985, on the EMI record label.
760. Who had originally recorded and had a hit with the song, back in 1964?

761. The front cover of which book, edited by Kerry Juby and first published by Omnibus Press in 1986, shows a close-up photograph of David with his right pupil seemingly dilated, instead of his left? No-one had noticed that the photograph had somehow been reversed during production.

762. Which theme song to the upcoming new film of the same name, did David release as a single, on the Virgin record label, in March 1986? The film was a musical tribute to the 1950s.

763. Released in April 1986, which was the first of two films released that year in which David appeared?
764. What's the connection between the film and David's 1984 extended music video film, **Jazzin' For Blue Jean**?
765. Who starred as the leading lady, Crepe Suzette?
766. Which character did David play?

ALL MY ~~IDIOT~~ 1500 QUESTIONS

767. Who wrote the novel of the same name, from which the film was adapted?
768. Other than the title track itself, which two other songs did David contribute to the soundtrack album?

769. Which new track, written for his second film of the year, did David release as a single in June 1986, on the EMI record label? The B side was an instrumental version of *Underground*.

770. First released in the US in June 1986, what was the second film in which David appeared that year?
771. Who directed the film?
772. Which character did David play?
773. Who was the young actress who played alongside David in the role of Sarah Williams?
774. The film was based on conceptual designs by Brian Froud, whose own son played the baby in the film. Name the baby.
775. Who, of Monty Python fame, was responsible for the film's screenplay?
776. What were the five songs written and recorded by David that featured on the soundtrack album released in June 1986, on the EMI record label?

777. What was David's next single, released in October 1986, on the Virgin record label? The track was taken from a Raymond Briggs film of the same name.
778. Which Turkish multi-instrumentalist co-wrote the track with David?

the 1980s

779. Which Iggy Pop album was released in October 1986 on the A&M record label, having been co-produced by David?

780. Prior to the release of the upcoming new album, which track from it became the lead single when it was released in March 1987, on the EMI record label?
781. Name the track that was on the B side, but ultimately failed to make it to the album.

782. Name David's 17th studio album, released in April 1987, on the EMI record label.
783. The title track on the album was written about David's relationship with whom?
784. Which of the following musicians did not feature on the album?
    a) Carlos Alomar
    b) Lenny Pickett
    c) Carmine Rojas
    d) Tony Thompson
785. On which track did American actor Mickey Rourke contribute vocals?
786. Which track disappeared from all future reissues of the album due to David's dislike of it?
787. Who co-produced the album with David?
788. Which of Iggy Pop's songs was covered on the album?
789. Solve the following anagrams to identify the two album tracks:-
    a) *Rory Fumed About*
    b) *Kevin Owns Elroy*

ALL MY ~~IDIOT~~ 1500 QUESTIONS

790. Which old school friend renewed his association with David, playing guitar on both the album and on the upcoming world tour?
791. Which track about nuclear devastation was in part inspired by the Chernobyl Disaster that occurred a year earlier?
792. Who on the album, played mellotron, moog synthesiser, harmonica and tambourine?

793. Which soft drinks company sponsored the upcoming world tour?
794. With whom did David appear in a TV commercial to promote the soft drink?
795. Which of David's compositions was played during the commercial, albeit with different lyrics written specifically for it?

796. What was the name of the 1987 theatrical Worldwide Concert Tour?
797. Following a handful of promotional press shows in North America, Europe and Oceania, the world tour got under way in May 1987, in which country?
798. Which of David's songs did his dancers perform at the very start of each show, prior to David making his entrance on to the stage?
799. Who was the female dancer who was 'planted' in the front row of the audience and then pulled up onto stage to dance with David during *Bang Bang*? She subsequently became David's girlfriend for a while.
800. By what name was dancer Craig Allen Rothwell otherwise known?
801. Who played bass guitar on the tour?

the 1980s

802. What was the name of the British lighting engineer who sadly fell to his death from scaffolding before a show in Florence, Italy, in June 1987?
803. Which four British venues were played on the tour?
804. As with the 'Diamond Dogs' tour of 1974, who choreographed the shows?
805. In which Australian city were shows recorded for a VHS video release the following year?

806. Name the second track on the album that also became the second single to be taken from it, when released in June 1987, on the EMI record label.
807. As with the previous single, the B side had not appeared on the album. Name the B side.

808. Which track became the third and final single from the latest album, released in August 1987 on the EMI record label? *'87 And Cry* was its B side.
809. Which long serving band member co-wrote the single with David?

810. At which London theatre, in July 1988, did David perform at the ICA fundraising event, 'Intruders At The Palace'?
811. Which of his own songs did he perform?
812. Who played guitar for the performance and in doing so, started a working relationship with David that would last more than ten years?
813. What was the name of the Canadian dance company with whom David performed?
814. Who were the two members of that dance company?

113

ALL MY ~~IDIOT~~ 1500 QUESTIONS

815. Released in the US in August 1988, name the epic religious drama film in which David appeared.
816. Who directed the film?
817. Which character did David play?
818. Which American actor played the part of Jesus?
819. Who, of Genesis and *Sledgehammer* fame, wrote music for the film?

820. By the end of the decade, David had formed which British-American hard rock supergroup?
821. Name the other three members of the band.

822. Name the band's 1st studio album, released in May 1989, on the EMI record label.
823. Who co-produced the album with the band?
824. Solve the following anagrams to identify the two album tracks:-
    a) Dodge Hunter
    b) Tin Arcade
825. Name the first track on the album; it was also the first track they recorded together.
826. Which two tracks appeared on the CD release of the album, but were omitted from the vinyl?
827. By what name was the track *Video Crime,* incorrectly listed on both the vinyl album sleeve track listing and on the vinyl LP itself? The track was correctly listed on the CD version of the album.
828. Which John Lennon track was covered on the album?
829. At which studios in Switzerland did recording first take place, before later moving to Compass Point Studios in Nassau?

the 1980s

830. Which two tracks on the album gave writing credits to all four band members?
831. Which non-band member played additional guitar on the album?
832. Which Japanese photographer took the album cover photograph?

833. Tin Machine played a live unannounced show in Nassau, in May 1989, before later that month performing at the 'Coca-Cola International Rock Awards', in New York. Which track did they perform at the awards ceremony?

834. When the band went out on tour in June 1989, Kevin Armstrong joined them to play additional guitar. Prior to working with Tin Machine, when and at which event had Kevin previously worked with David?
835. The tour only comprised twelve small venue shows, in six different countries. It started in the US and finished in the UK, but which four European countries hosted the tour in between?
836. Which Bob Dylan track did the band add to their live repertoire?
837. Which track from the album did they perform live, country and western style?

838. *Heaven's In Here* was released as a promo only single but three other tracks from the album were released as official 7" singles during 1989. Listed below are the B sides, together with their release dates, name the A sides.

a) *Sacrifice Yourself (June)*
b) *Maggie's Farm (Live) (September)*
c) *Baby Can Dance (Live) (October)*

Figure 11: 1980s' Tours' Programmes and Tickets from Author's Collection

the 1980s
233 Answers

606. *Play It Safe*
607. 8th February 1980
608. Alabama Song
609. Heroes
610. Crystal Jun Rock
611. Crystal Japan
612. Move On
613. David Mallet
614. Steve Strange
615. No. 1 – the first UK No. 1 since *Space Oddity*
616. The Elephant Man
617. Jack Hofsiss
618. Joseph (John) Merrick
619. Philip Anglim
620. Denver and Chicago
621. Scary Monsters (and Super Creeps)
622. Tom Verlaine's *Kingdom Come*
623. Because You're Young

624. Michi Hirota
625. Natasha Kornilof
626. a) *Up The Hill Backwards*
    b) *Teenage Wildlife*
627. Roy Bittan
628. *Tired Of My Life*
629. Tony Visconti
630. *Fashion*
631. *I Am A Laser*
632. *Fashion*
633. John Lennon
634. **The Best Of Bowie**
635. *Because You're Young*
636. Lulu
637. The Polecats
638. *Up The Hill Backwards*
639. Christiane F. – Wir Kinder Vom Bahnhof Zoo
640. *Station To Station*
641. Natja Brunckhorst
642. Only Fools And Horses
643. Free Spirit
644. *Under Pressure*
645. Mountain Studios, Montreux
646. John Deacon
647. **Hot Space**
648. *Wild Is The Wind*
649. **Changestwobowie**
650. 1970
651. Baal
652. Herbert Beerholm Baal
653. Alan Clarke

the 1980s

654. *Ballad Of The Adventurers, The Drowned Girl* and *The Dirty Song*
655. *Cat People (Putting Out Fire)*
656. Giorgio Moroder
657. Paul Schrader
658. *Ziggy Stardust*
659. *Peace On Earth/Little Drummer Boy*
660. Fashions
661. Lausanne
662. EMI
663. Claridges Hotel in Mayfair
664. The Hunger
665. Whitley Streiber
666. John Blaylock
667. Catherine Deneuve and Susan Sarandon
668. Tony Scott
669. *Let's Dance*
670. David Mallet
671. Carinda
672. Terry Roberts and Jolene King
673. **Let's Dance**
674. Nile Rodgers
675. *China Girl, Criminal World* and *Cat People (Putting Out Fire)*
676. New York
677. Greg Gorman
678. David played no instruments – the first album on which he only contributed vocals
679. Stevie Ray Vaughan
680. a) *Modern Love*
    b) *Ricochet*
681. *China Girl*

682. Metro
683. Omar Hakim and Tony Thompson
684. Brussels
685. The Serious Moonlight Tour
686. Carlos Alomar
687. Denis O'Regan
688. Earl Slick
689. Jim was Head of Security
690. Brixton Neighbourhood Community Association
691. Montreal
692. Pacific National Exhibition Coliseum
693. Mick Ronson
694. *Cracked Actor*
695. Frank and George Simms
696. David performed the Lennon song, *Imagine*
697. A film called **Ricochet** that had been shot during the Far East leg of the tour (the end of the tour) and released commercially a year later on VHS video
698. Merry Christmas Mr. Lawrence
699. The Cook Islands (New Zealand was also used)
700. Nagisa Oshima
701. Jack 'Strafer' Celliers
702. Tom Conti
703. Ryuichi Sakamoto
704. Geeling Ng
705. Marlon Brando
706. Yellowbeard
707. The Shark (Henson)
708. *Modern Love*
709. **Ziggy Stardust: The Motion Picture**
710. Ken Pitt
711. **Love You Till Tuesday**

712. 1984
713. A View To A Kill
714. Jazzin' For Blue Jean
715. Julien Temple
716. Screaming Lord Byron
717. Vic
718. Louise Scott
719. Ian Ellis
720. Tonight
721. Canada
722. Hugh Padgham
723. Loving The Alien and *Blue Jean*
724. Tina Turner
725. a) *Loving The Alien*
b) *Tumble And Twirl*
726. b) Mike Garson didn't
727. Dancing With The Big Boys
728. Tonight and *Neighborhood Threat*
729. The Beach Boys
730. Mike Haggerty
731. The Snowman
732. China Girl
733. Michael Jackson Video Vanguard Award (Lifetime Achievement Award)
734. Tonight
735. David didn't sing any line - but he did contribute a message to the B side
736. Terry committed suicide, stepping out into the path of a train
737. The Pat Metheny Group
738. This Is Not America
739. The Falcon And The Snowman

740. Best Video, Short Form (later renamed as Best Music Video)
741. Into The Night
742. John Landis
743. Colin Morris
744. Jeff Goldblum and Michelle Pfeiffer
745. Tina Turner
746. Bryan Adams
747. *Loving The Alien*
748. David Mallet
749. Live Aid
750. Prince and Princess of Wales (Charles and Diana)
751. Status Quo
752. Queen
753. *TVC15, Rebel Rebel, Modern Love* and *Heroes*
754. *Five Years*
755. *Drive*
756. Clare Hurst
757. Thomas Dolby
758. Mick Jagger
759. *Dancing In The Street*
760. Martha and the Vandellas
761. In Other Words
762. *Absolute Beginners*
763. Absolute Beginners
764. Both were directed by Julian Temple
765. Patsy Kensit
766. Vendice Partners
767. Colin MacInnes
768. *That's Motivation* and *Volare*
769. *Underground*
770. Labyrinth

the 1980s

771. Jim Henson
772. Jareth The Goblin King
773. Jennifer Connelly
774. Toby Froud (Toby Williams in the film)
775. Terry Jones
776. *Underground, Magic Dance, Chilly Down, As The World Falls Down* and *Within You*
777. *When The Wind Blows*
778. Erdal Kizilcay
779. **Blah Blah Blah**
780. *Day-In Day-Out*
781. *Julie*
782. **Never Let Me Down**
783. PA Coco Schwab
784. d) Tony Thompson didn't
785. *Shining Star (Makin' My Love)*
786. *Too Dizzy*
787. David Richards
788. *Bang Bang*
789. a) *Beat Of Your Drum*
     b) *New York's In Love*
790. Peter Frampton
791. *Time Will Crawl*
792. David Bowie
793. Pepsi Cola
794. Tina Turner
795. *Modern Love*
796. The Glass Spider Tour
797. Holland
798. *Up The Hill Backwards*
799. Melissa Hurley
800. Spazz Attack

ALL MY ~~IDIOT~~ 1500 QUESTIONS

801. Carmine Rojas
802. Michael Clark
803. Wembley Stadium, Cardiff Arms Park, Roker Park in Sunderland and Maine Road in Manchester
804. Toni Basil
805. Sydney
806. Time Will Crawl
807. Girls
808. Never Let Me Down
809. Carlos Alomar
810. Dominion Theatre
811. Look Back In Anger
812. Reeves Gabrels
813. La La La Human Steps
814. Louise Lecavalier and Edouard Lock
815. The Last Temptation of Christ
816. Martin Scorsese
817. Pontius Pilate
818. William Dafoe
819. Peter Gabriel
820. Tin Machine
821. Reeves Gabrels, Hunt Sales and Tony Fox Sales
822. Tin Machine
823. Tim Palmer
824. a) Under The God
    b) I Can't Read
825. Heaven's In Here
826. Run and *Sacrifice Yourself*
827. Video Crimes (plural)
828. Working Class Hero
829. Mountain Studios in Montreux
830. Tin Machine and *Prisoner Of Love*

124

the 1980s

831. Kevin Armstrong
832. Masayoshi Sukita
833. *Heaven's In Here*
834. 1985 at Live Aid
835. Denmark, Germany, The Netherlands and France
836. *Maggie's Farm*
837. *Bus Stop*
838. a) *Under The God*
    b) *Tin Machine*
    c) *Prisoner Of Love*

Figure 12: Selection of items from Author's Collection, featuring works and publications from the 1980s

ALL MY ~~IDIOT~~ 1500 QUESTIONS

the 1990s

Figure 13: Alamy Stock Photo

the 1990s
262 Questions

839. What was the title of the compilation album consisting of David's popular hits, released in March 1990 on the EMI record label? It was released partly in support of the upcoming world tour.

840. Billed as a Greatest Hits Tour, what was the name of the Worldwide Concert Tour that started in March 1990, in Canada?

841. Who joined the tour as Music Director and lead guitarist, having previously worked with David on the 1978 world tour and on the **Lodger** album?

842. Who co-conceived the tour, and was Artistic Director?

843. David announced that a telephone poll would in part at least, determine the setlist. Which music magazine ran a spoof campaign in an effort to get David to include *The Laughing Gnome* in the setlist?

844. Which three band members played bass, keyboards and drums respectively, on the tour?

ALL MY ~~IDIOT~~ 1500 QUESTIONS

845. At which UK venue in August 1990, was the show recorded for a BBC Radio One broadcast?
846. In which South American country did the tour conclude, in September 1990?

847. To coincide with the tour, remixes of one of David's early songs were released as a single, in March 1990, on the EMI record label? The original version had appeared on the **Young Americans** album, in 1975. Name the new single.
848. Various remixes of the track were released in various packaging and various formats. Complete the names of these remixes of the new track:-
    a) G _ _ _ Mix
    b) H _ _ _ _ Mix
    c) H _ _ H _ _ Mix
    d) B _ _ _ _ B _ _ _ Mix
    e) Q _ _ _ _ L _ _ _ _ _ _ _ ' _ R _ _ Version
849. On which film's soundtrack album, also released in March 1990, did the new single also appear?

850. At which Grosvenor House awards ceremony, in April 1990, did David win an award for 'Outstanding Contribution To British Music'?

851. Adrian Belew's album **Young Lions** was released in May 1990 on the Atlantic record label. Which song on the album did David write and contribute vocals? He also performed it throughout the 'Sound and Vision' world tour.

the 1990s

852. Which American rapper had a hit single in July 1990, the bassline of which had been based on *Under Pressure*, the collaboration between David and Queen?
853. What was the title of this rapper's single? It went on to top the UK charts.

854. David and Iman were introduced to each other in October 1990, by which mutual hairdresser and friend?

855. 'The Crossing' was an Australian romantic drama film, released in October 1990, and starred Russell Crowe. A version of which Tin Machine track appeared on the accompanying soundtrack album?

856. In which American crime comedy film, released in May 1991, did David appear?
857. Which character did David play?
858. Who played opposite David in the role of Lucy?
859. Three of the following, all had small cameo roles in the film. Which one didn't?
    a) Iman
    b) Iggy Pop
    c) Hunt Sales
    d) Julian Lennon

860. Broadcast in the US in July 1991, what was the name of the American sitcom in which David appeared, in an episode entitled 'The Second Greatest Story Ever Told: Parts 1 & 2'?
861. Which character did David play?

862. Name the compilation album, released in 1991 on the Rhino label, which made an attempt to compile a comprehensive collection of David's pre-Deram material between 1964 and 1966.

863. The album introduced five previously unreleased early tracks from Shel Talmy's collection. Fill in the blanks to complete the five song titles :-
    a) That's W____ M_ H____ I_
    b) I W___ M_ B___ B___
    c) Bars O_ T__ C_____ J___
    d) I'll F_____ Y__
    e) Glad I'__ G__ N_____

864. Broadcast in August 1991, on which BBC music and comedy TV show presented by Curtis and Ishmael, did Tin Machine appear, performing two new songs?

865. Which two new songs did the band perform?

866. Broadcast on BBC One in August 1991, on whose chat show did Tin Machine appear?

867. Which track did the band perform?

868. David's suit for that performance was a bright shade of which colour?

869. Ahead of the upcoming new Tin Machine album, which track was released as the lead single in August 1991, on the Victory Music record label? The B side was 'Amlapura (Indonesian version)'.

870. Name Tin Machine's 2nd studio album, released in September 1991, on the Victory Music record label.

the 1990s

871. The album was produced by Tin Machine and Tim Palmer but who provided additional production on the track *One Shot*?
872. Which Bryan Ferry song was covered on the album?
873. Which two track names on the album start with the letter '*A*'?
874. For which two tracks did Hunt Sales provide lead vocals?
875. According to the inner sleeve notes, Reeves Gabrels was credited with lead and rhythm guitar, backing vocals, drano, organ, and what else?
876. Which track on the album was about child prostitution in the Far East? The idea for the song came about after the then wife of Reeves Gabrels, American journalist Sara Terry, wrote a magazine article about the subject.
877. Solve the following anagrams to identify the two album tracks:-
    a) *Edgy Boredom*
    b) *A Nutty Cloak*
878. Name the hidden instrumental track that appeared at the end of the album.
879. Which track became the second single from the album when released in October 1991, on the Victory Music record label? The 7" vinyl included an extended version of *You Belong In Rock n' Roll* on its B side.
880. Which photographer and illustrator created the album's cover artwork?

881. The new Tin Machine Worldwide Concert Tour began in October 1991, in Milan but in which Irish city had

the band been rehearsing and performing warm up shows, some two months earlier?

882. What was the name of the tour?
883. Who joined the band on stage to provide additional guitar?
884. The band took time out to be interviewed in a one hour special, for the 'MTV Post Modern' programme, in October 1991. Which presenter interviewed the band?
885. At which venue in Germany, in October 1991, was the concert filmed for a VHS video release the following year?
886. Which Pixies cover did the band often include in the setlist?
887. The tour reached the UK in November 1991. Which one of the following, did not stage a show?
    a) Brixton
    b) Liverpool
    c) Sunderland
    d) Wolverhampton

888. Broadcast in November 1991, Tin Machine appeared on the US late night TV show, 'Saturday Night Live'. Which young actor hosted the show, introducing the band twice?
889. Which two songs were performed and broadcast?

890. Backed by the track *Hammerhead*, which was the third and final track from the **Tin Machine II** album to be released as a single, in November 1991, on the Victory Music record label?

the 1990s

891. Released in December 1991, who played the part of Martia in the film 'Star Trek VI: The Undiscovered Country'?

892. An *808 Gift Mix*, an *808 'lectric Blue Remix Instrumental*, a *David Richards Remix* and the original version, of which track from **Low**, all appeared on a US 12" vinyl single released in December 1991, on the Tommy Boy/Rykodisc record label?

893. David began work on his next album, at the time of the Los Angeles Riots in April 1992. Inspiring David to write the title track and reflect on racial harmony, who was the African-American at the centre of the police brutality victimisation?

894. At which concert for Aids awareness did David appear in April 1992, at Wembley Stadium?
895. With whom did David duet on *Under Pressure* ("That Dress !")?
896. For a performance of which song was David joined on stage by Ian Hunter and Mick Ronson?
897. What was the last track David performed before unexpectedly falling to his knees to recite the Lord's Prayer?

898. Where, on the 24th April 1992, eighteen months after they'd first met, did David and Iman get married?
899. Where, on the 6th June 1992, was the union then solemnized?

ALL MY ~~IDIOT~~ 1500 QUESTIONS

900. First released in May 1992 at the Cannes Film Festival, in which film did David appear as an FBI Agent?
901. What was the name of David's character?
902. Who directed the film?

903. Who in 1992, composed his **Symphony No. 1**, based on David's 1977 **Low** album?
904. The symphony consisted of three movements; *Subterraneans*, *Some Are* and which other?

905. A Tin Machine concert from Germany in October 1991, was released as a video film in July 1992. What was the title of the video release?
906. Which Moody Blues cover appeared in the video?
907. Who sang lead vocals on the cover?

908. David's first new single following the dissolution of Tin Machine, was released in August 1992, on the Warner Bros. record label. Taken from the soundtrack of the film 'Cool World', what was the name of the single?
909. Returning to production duties after nearly ten years away, who produced the single?

910. In which British comedy show, written by Dick Clement and Ian La Frenais, did David appear as himself in an episode called 'Ivory Tower'? The episode aired in January 1993.

the 1990s

911. Published in January 1993, whose kiss and tell book was entitled, 'Backstage Passes: Life On the Wild Side with David Bowie'?

912. Which track from the upcoming new album was released as the lead single, in March 1993, on the Arista record label? The song loosely dealt with David's feelings for his schizophrenic half-brother Terry, who had committed suicide some eight years earlier in 1985.

913. Who shot the accompanying music video?

914. Name David's 18th studio album, released in April 1993, on the Arista record label.
915. As well as Mountain Studios in Montreux, the album was also partly recorded in which two US cities?
916. Who co-produced the album with David?
917. David was a huge fan of Scott Walker. Which of Scott's tracks did he cover on the album?
918. Solve the following anagrams to identify the two album tracks:-
    a) *Nightgown Deeds*
    b) *Monolithic Dagger*
919. Who made a special guest appearance playing guitar on the cover, *I Feel Free*?
920. Which pianist worked again with David for the first time since **Young Americans**, contributing to the track, *Looking For Lester*?
921. Which David namesake and American jazz trumpet player contributed extensively to the album?
922. Which track was written by Tahra Mint Hembara?
923. Name the instrumental track that opened the album.

ALL MY ~~IDIOT~~ 1500 QUESTIONS

924. Which Morrissey song did David cover?

925. Cited as the guitarist who was most instrumental in David's rise to fame in the 1970s, who died of liver cancer on 29th April 1993?

926. In May 1993, David was filmed performing six tracks from the latest album as well as talking freely about the album, and much more. Released as a VHS music video in 1993, and simply entitled **Black Tie White Noise**, who directed the one hour production shot in Los Angeles?

927. Who provided guest vocals on the single *Black Tie White Noise*, released in June 1993, on the Arista record label?

928. What was the title of the one hour 1993 MTV programme in which David sat, talked and personally introduced ten of his own most popular music videos?

929. Which track was released as a single in October 1993, on the Arista record label? It was backed by *Looking For Lester*.

930. Which American rock band recorded a session at the Sony Music Studios in New York, for the 'MTV Unplugged' show, in November 1993? They performed their version of *The Man Who Sold The World*.

931. Released in 1993 by Picture Music International, what was the name of the VHS video tape that

the 1990s

consisted of twenty five official music videos made by David between 1972 and 1990?

932. Who designed the ice blue satin suit for the *Life On Mars?* music video?
933. Which American actress had flown from New York to San Francisco to appear in the music video for *The Jean Genie*?
934. Directed by David Mallet, which music video was shot in black and white?
935. Who directed the *Space Oddity* music video?

936. David contributed a soundtrack album to which four-part TV serial, broadcast by the BBC in November 1993? The serial was based on the novel of the same name by Hanif Kureishi.
937. The theme song to the series was released as a single in November 1993 on the Arista record label. From which track on **The Man Who Sold The World** album did David lift the outro lyric, *zane zane zane ouvrez le chien*?
938. Who gets a 'played guitar' credit on the *Rock Mix* of the title track?
939. The title of which track is an anagram of Hanif Kureishi?

940. Thirty seven singles released by David between 1969 and 1993 were collectively released as a 2-CD compilation album by EMI, in November 1993. What was the title of the album?

941. World Aids Day is recognised on the 1st December, each year. In 1993, in the presence of Princess Diana,

David presented the very first 'Concert For Hope' from Wembley Arena. He didn't perform himself, but which three artists did he introduce to perform?

942. What was the name of Mick Ronson's final solo album on which David collaborated, released posthumously in May 1994 on the Epic record label?
943. On which Bob Dylan cover did David provide the vocal?
944. Which song written by David, appeared on the album as the last track?

945. In June 1994, the first two Mick Ronson solo albums were released as a 2-CD compilation entitled **Only After Dark**, on the Golden Years record label. Mick's cover of which track from **The Rise and Fall of Ziggy Stardust and The Spiders from Mars**, appeared on the compilation album as a bonus track?

946. Which fashion model and actress played the part of Nina Blackstone in the American comedy thriller 'Exit To Eden', released in October 1994?

947. With which British textile design company did David collaborate during 1995, to create a series of wallpapers inspired by modern psychology and mythical figures?

948. David sold his purpose built 'Britannia Bay House', in the mid-1990s, to business tycoon and poet Felix Dennis. On which small private island in the nation

the 1990s

of Saint Vincent and the Grenadines in the West Indies, was the house located?

949. Which track from the upcoming new album, was released as the lead single in September 1995, on the Arista record label?

950. The 'Outside' Worldwide Concert Tour started in September 1995, in which Connecticut city?
951. Who played drums on the tour?
952. Which American rock band supported the American leg of the tour?
953. Which artist was the support act for the European leg of the tour but unexpectedly withdrew after just nine shows?
954. Who was back in the fold, playing lead guitar?
955. Who became David's touring bass player for the first time?

956. Name David's 19th studio album, released in September 1995, on the Arista record label.
957. At nearly 75 minutes, the album was easily David's longest studio album. How many tracks made up the album?
958. Which track on the album had originally appeared, albeit a different recording, on the **Buddha Of Suburbia** soundtrack album released in 1993?
959. Solve the following anagrams to identify the two album tracks:-
    a) *Gear Minded*
    b) *Payable School*

ALL MY ~~IDIOT~~ 1500 QUESTIONS

960. Who worked with David again as writer and co-producer, for the first time since **Lodger**?
961. The concept album concerned the inhabitants of which fictional town?
962. Name the detective who investigated the murder of the 14 year old girl, Baby Grace Blue.
963. The album cover was a painting composed by whom?
964. Which multi-instrumentalist played bass and keyboards on the album?
965. Which track on the album referenced Ramona, Paddy and Miranda?
966. Complete the track titles of these three segues :-
    a) *Segue:* N _ _ _ _ _   A _ _ _ _
    b) *Segue:* R _ _ _ _ _   A. S _ _ _ _
    c) *Segue:* A _ _ _ _ _ _   T _ _ _ _ _ _ _ _ _

967. Which album was released in 1995 having been originally recorded around 1973 by David's backing singers, Ava Cherry, Geoff MacCormack and Jason Guess?
968. By what group name were the singers collectively known?

969. Who, in 1995, interviewed David for a VH-1 channel programme called 'VH-1 to 1'?

970. David contributed a version of *I'm Afraid Of Americans*, to which movie soundtrack album, released in September 1995?

971. In November 1995, the second track to be released from the new album as a single, was *Strangers When*

the 1990s

We Meet. The B side was a live version of which 1970s track?

972. At the 'MTV Europe Music Awards' in Paris, in November 1995, David appeared in a pre-show interview with Ray Cokes, featuring puppets Zig and Zag, before being introduced to the stage by Jean Paul Gautier. David performed a new version of which old classic?

973. David made the first of three TV appearances on the BBC's 'Later With Jools' music show in December 1995. As well as sitting at the piano to be interviewed, which three tracks were performed and broadcast?

974. Presented by Mark Radcliffe and Jo Whiley in December 1995, on which Channel 4 TV music show did David appear?

975. Although bootleg copies of the entire set exist, which four songs were broadcast?

976. David appeared at the 'Big Twix Mix – The Greatest Party In The World', in December 1995. At which UK venue did the show take place?

977. By whom was David inducted into the 'Rock and Roll Hall Of Fame', in January 1996?

978. Who accepted the award on David's behalf?

979. Broadcast in January 1996, which BBC Radio DJ, presenter and journalist did Michael Aspel surprise with the big red 'This Is Your Life' book? David was a

ALL MY ~~IDIOT~~ 1500 QUESTIONS

contributor and thanked the subject of the show for his faith and for his help in the early days.

980. Which award did David receive at the 16th 'Brit Awards' ceremony, in February 1996?
981. Who introduced and presented David with the award?
982. With whom did David perform *Hallo Spaceboy* at the event?
983. Which two other songs did David also perform for the occasion?

984. *Hallo Spaceboy* featuring The Pet Shop Boys, was released as a single in February 1996. The CD single released in the UK also contained a radio edit of *The Hearts Filthy Lesson* as well as which two live tracks, both recorded at the 'Big Twix Mix' show in Birmingham at the end of 1995?

985. At which summer festival in Stratford-Upon-Avon did David appear, in July 1996?

986. The second symphony by Philip Glass, based on David's work, was **Symphony No. 4** and it was composed in 1996. On which of David's albums was the symphony based?

987. First released in the US, in August 1996, in which film did David appear about the life of an American postmodernist/neoexpressionist artist?
988. Which character did David play?
989. Who directed the film?

the 1990s

990. Which of David's close personal friends also starred in the film, playing the part of Albert Milo?
991. The soundtrack album included Iggy Pop's *Lust For Life* as well as which track from David's **1.Outside** album?

992. Released in September 1996 on David's official website, which track became the first ever downloadable single by a major artist?

993. At which benefit concerts in California did David appear for two consecutive nights in October 1996?
994. Which two regular band members of the day accompanied David on stage for both performances?
995. With which song did David open both performances?
996. The concerts were an annual event, but who organized them each year?

997. Filmed at Madison Square Garden and broadcast in October 1996, on which VH-1 awards show did David perform *Fashion* and *Little Wonder*?

998. Which former politician turned author, published a book called 'David Bowie – Living on the Brink' in November 1996, some 22 years after he'd published one of the first ever books about David, simply entitled 'The David Bowie Story'?

999. At which venue on the 9th January 1997, did David and guests perform a concert as part of his 50th Birthday celebrations?

ALL MY ~~IDIOT~~ 1500 QUESTIONS

1000. With which artist did David perform *Scary Monsters (And Super Creeps)* and *Fashion*?
1001. Which track from **Hunky Dory** did David perform with The Cure's Robert Smith?
1002. Who did David introduce to the stage as the "King of New York himself"?
1003. As well as performing *Queen Bitch*, which three songs written by Lou Reed did he and David perform?
1004. As the birthday cake was brought to the stage, which band member led the singing of *Happy Birthday*?
1005. Which guest performed *The Jean Genie* with David?

1006. Released by Big Eye Film & Television Ltd in January 1997, who interviewed David for a documentary entitled 'An Earthling at 50'?

1007. *Little Wonder* from the upcoming new album, was released as a single (in various mixes), in January 1997, on the Parlophone record label. Who directed the accompanying music video?

1008. To which soundtrack album, released in February 1997 and produced by Trent Reznor, did David contribute the track *I'm Deranged*?

1009. Name David's 20th studio album, released in February 1997, on the Arista record label.
1010. In which two countries was the album recorded?
1011. Which New York-based record producer and engineer worked with David for the first time, receiving co-producer credits?

the 1990s

1012. What words in brackets complete the track name, *Battle For Britain*?
1013. The track *Seven Years In Tibet* was inspired by a 1952 book of the same name, by which Austrian author?
1014. Solve the following anagrams to identify the two album tracks:-
    a) *Adrian Mariam Offices*
    b) *Athens Doughtily Holds Out*
1015. Which track closed the album?
1016. Which of these drummers played on the album?
    a) Zachory Alford
    b) Sterling Campbell
    c) Aynsley Dunbar
    d) Mike Levesque
1017. Who designed the Union Jack frock coat which David wore for the front cover photoshoot?
1018. Which American musician played bass on the album? Although she'd been a part of the 1995 world tour, this was the first time she'd contributed to one of David's studio albums.
1019. For which track did David say his starting point was Snow White and the Seven Dwarfs, and he wrote a line for each of the dwarfs' names?

1020. Introduced by Neve Campbell in February 1997, on which American late night TV show did David perform *Little Wonder* and *Scary Monsters (And Super Creeps)*?

1021. Which Hollywood Boulevard honour did David receive in February 1997?

ALL MY ~~IDIOT~~ 1500 QUESTIONS

1022. Which track from the **Earthling** album was released as a single in April 1997, on the BMG record label? The basic riff for the track had been used back in 1970 on the track, *The Supermen.*

1023. What was the name of the compilation album released in June 1997 on the Deram record label, consisting of the material David had previously recorded with the label, between 1966 and 1968?

1024. Which track did David and Gail Ann Dorsey write, record and contribute to the **Long Live Tibet** charity album, released in June 1997?

1025. In which European country did the 'Earthling' Worldwide Concert Tour start, in June 1997?
1026. With which track from **Hunky Dory** did David often open shows, initially just himself and guitar?
1027. Which Laurie Anderson song was performed on tour?
1028. Who sang lead vocals on the Laurie Anderson cover?
1029. At which festival in Stratford-Upon-Avon did David headline, in July 1997?
1030. The night before his headline performance, David and the band played a secret gig at the Radio One Dance tent, under what pseudonym?
1031. For which MTV programme was the Port Chester, New York show recorded in October 1997?
1032. In which South American country did the tour end, in November 1997?

the 1990s

1033. In the summer of 1997 whilst in Bermuda, which John Lennon cover did David record at Yoko Ono's request, originally intended for inclusion on a Lennon Tribute Album?

1034. Which track, released in August 1997 on 7" vinyl, on the BMG record label, included a mandarin version of the same track, on its B side?

1035. Why were David and Brian Eno credited on the Blur track *M.O.R.*, released as a single in September 1997, on the Parlophone record label?

1036. Which track from the **Earthling** album was released as a single in October 1997, on the Virgin record label? The single was co-produced by Trent Reznor.

1037. Which Bowie/Gabrels song from the first **Tin Machine** album appeared on **The Ice Storm** soundtrack album, released in October 1997 on the Velvel record label? The film starred Kevin Kline and Sigourney Weaver.

1038. At which magazine awards ceremony did David perform a full headline set to close proceedings, in October 1997?

1039. Filmed at the Radio City Music Hall in New York, with which track from the **Low** album did David open his set?

1040. Which charity single, featuring David and many other artists, reached No. 1 in the UK charts when it

ALL MY ~~IDIOT~~ 1500 QUESTIONS

was released on the Chrysalis record label in aid of 'Children In Need', in November 1997?

1041. Who had written and recorded the original version of the song, back in 1972?

1042. Released in November 1997, **Closure** was the first VHS video album by American rock band Nine Inch Nails. On which track did David contribute vocals?

1043. What was the name of the six track promotional CD album that was distributed by GQ magazine in the November 1997 issue?

1044. David launched his own Internet Service Provider, initially in North America, in September 1998. What was it called?

1045. An anagram of 'Isolar', by what name was David known in the chat room?

1046. Known as 'Total Blam Blam' who ultimately maintained 'Bowienet' as well as David's official website, www.davidbowie.com?

1047. Who narrated the 'VH-1 Legends' documentary that featured David as its subject in September 1998?

1048. Which film directed by Todd Haynes, shared its name with one of David's early songs and was released in October 1998?

1049. The film was set in the glam rock era of the 1970s and characters bore a striking resemblance to those around David at the time. What was the name of the

148

the 1990s

prominent Ziggy Stardust-like character, played by Jonathan Rhys Meyers?

1050. Who played the part of the Pantomime Dame in the film?

1051. Which song did David record for an Aids awareness album, released in October 1998, on the Verve/Antilles record label. The compilation album was titled **Red Hot + Rhapsody: The Gershwin Groove**.

1052. Which new song did David write for the animation film soundtrack, **The Rugrats Movie**, released in November 1998? Ultimately, the track was not used.

1053. First released in Italy, in December 1998, what was the original name of the spaghetti western film in which David appeared?
1054. By what name was the film known when released some time later in the US?
1055. Which character did David play?
1056. Who directed the movie?

1057. With which English rock band did David take to the stage to perform, at the 19th 'Brit Awards', at the London Arena, in February 1999?
1058. Which Marc Bolan song did they perform?

1059. In which film, released in March 1999, did David appear alongside Goldie and Rachel Shelley?
1060. What different title did the film have when released in the US?

149

ALL MY ~~IDIOT~~ 1500 QUESTIONS

1061. What was the name of the aging gangster character played by David?

1062. David received an Honorary Doctorate, in May 1999, from which music college in Boston?

1063. Released in August 1999, on the Virgin record label, on which Placebo single did David contribute vocals?

1064. A version of a new track, *The Pretty Things Are Going To Hell*, was featured on which film's soundtrack album, released in August 1999?

1065. In August 1999, David was filmed performing a short set, interspersed with stories about his life, in front of a small audience in New York. For which VH1 TV programme was the session recorded?

1066. Which musician played in David's band for the last time, having first met back in 1987?

1067. Which track from the 1960s did David perform?

1068. Who were the two backing vocalists?

1069. Backed by *We All Go Through*, *No One Calls*, *We Shall Go To Town* and *1917*, on two separate CDs, which track taken from the upcoming new album was released as the lead single, in September 1999?

1070. Who directed the accompanying music video?

1071. First aired in September 1999, David became the host of which British/Canadian television horror series?

the 1990s

1072. David took over the role for Series Two of the show. Who had hosted Series One?

1073. Name David's 21st studio album, released in September 1999, on the Virgin record label.
1074. Who co-produced the album with David, as well as playing guitar?
1075. Solve the following anagrams to identify the two album tracks:-
   a) *Rose Fleming's Weapon*
   b) *Eighth Inseminator*
1076. From whose autobiography did the *Thursday's Child* title come?
1077. Who was the winner of the song contest conducted on 'Bowienet' to write lyrics for the track *What's Really Happening?*?
1078. Which track closed the album?
1079. In what capacity was Tim Bret Day involved in the album?
1080. As well as Sterling Campbell, who else played drums on the album?
1081. The album was partly recorded at the Seaview Studios in which British overseas territory, in the North Atlantic Ocean?
1082. At just over seven minutes, which was the longest track on the album?
1083. Which American singer-songwriter performed backing vocals on the album?

1084. In October 1999, David began a short mini tour to promote the **Hours** album. Who was Music Director

ALL MY ~~IDIOT~~ 1500 QUESTIONS

for the tour, as well as playing guitar and bass guitar in the band?

1085. The first show of the tour was at Wembley Stadium in aid of which anti-poverty initiative?

1086. The Wembley show was one of three shows worldwide, held simultaneously to raise money and awareness. In which two countries did the two other shows take place?

1087. David's short set at Wembley consisted of six songs, but only two of them were from the latest album. Which two?

1088. Who, for this show and the rest of the mini tour, had replaced Reeves Gabrels on guitar?

1089. Who were the two backing singers for the tour?

1090. Broadcast in October 1999, on which Channel 4 TV music show did David appear, performing *Rebel Rebel*, and *Survive*, as well as being interviewed?

1091. Who hosted the show and conducted the 'In the Chair' interview?

1092. What was the name of the computer adventure game, released for Microsoft Windows in October 1999, for which David and Reeves Gabrels had written music during the **Hours** album sessions?

1093. Which character did David play, in the game itself?

1094. David's wife, Iman, also served as a model for a 'bodyguard for hire' type of character in the game. What was the character name?

1095. Which track from the **Aladdin Sane** album did David perform live at the request of 'Mark & Lard', when he appeared on their BBC Radio One show in October 1999?

1096. Which top French Arts Honour was awarded to David, in October 1999, for his lifetime achievement in music?

1097. Name the limited edition album, released in November 1999, which was not commercially available and which could only be acquired by being subscribed to 'BowieNet'.

1098. The album was made up of individual tracks, all recorded live, predominantly during which tour?

1099. Broadcast in December 1999, who interviewed David for an episode of the BBC TV current affairs programme, 'Newsnight'?

1100. Broadcast in December 1999, on which BBC TV music show did David appear for a second time, performing *Ashes To Ashes*, *Something In The Air*, *Survive* and *Cracked Actor*?

ALL MY ~~IDIOT~~ 1500 QUESTIONS

Figure 14: Selection of items from Author's Collection, featuring works from the 1990s

the 1990s
262 Answers

839. Changesbowie
840. The Sound And Vision Tour
841. Adrian Belew
842. Edouard Lock of La La La Human Steps
843. NME
844. Erdal Kizilcay, Rick Fox and Michael Hodges
845. Milton Keynes Bowl
846. Argentina
847. Fame '90
848. a) Gass Mix
   b) House Mix
   c) Hip Hop Mix
   d) Bonus Beat Mix
   e) Queen Latifah's Rap Version
849. Pretty Woman
850. Ivor Novello Awards
851. Pretty Pink Rose
852. Vanilla Ice

853. *Ice Ice Baby*
854. Teddy Antolin
855. *Betty Wrong*
856. The Linguini Incident
857. Monte (British bartender)
858. Rosanna Arquette
859. b) Iggy Pop didn't
860. Dream On
861. Sir Roland Moorecock
862. Early On (1964 – 1966)
863. a) *That's Where My Heart Is*
    b) *I Want My Baby Back*
    c) *Bars Of The County Jail*
    d) *I'll Follow You*
    e) *Glad I've Got Nobody*
864. Paramount City
865. *You Belong In Rock n' Roll* and *Baby Universal*
866. Wogan
867. *You Belong In Rock n' Roll*
868. Lime Green
869. *You Belong In Rock n' Roll*
870. Tin Machine II
871. Hugh Padgham
872. *If There Is Something*
873. *Amlapura* and *A Big Hurt*
874. *Stateside* and *Sorry*
875. Vibrators
876. *Shopping For Girls*
877. a) *Goodbye Mr. Ed*
    b) *You Can't Talk*
878. *Hammerhead*
879. *Baby Universal*

880. Edward Bell
881. Dublin
882. It's My Life Tour
883. Eric Schermerhorn
884. Pip Dann
885. The Docks, Hamburg
886. Debaser
887. c) Sunderland didn't
888. Macaulay Culkin
889. Baby Universal and *If There Is Something*
890. One Shot
891. Iman
892. Sound And Vision
893. Rodney King
894. Freddie Mercury Tribute Concert
895. Annie Lennox
896. All The Young Dudes
897. Heroes
898. Lausanne, Switzerland
899. Florence, Italy
900. Twin Peaks - Fire Walk With Me
901. Phillip Jeffries
902. David Lynch
903. Philip Glass (also known as the Low symphony)
904. Warszawa
905. Oh Vey Baby: Tin Machine Live At The Docks
906. *Go Now* (The original was recorded by Bessie Banks in 1964, but the Moody Blues version with Denny Lainc on guitar and lead vocals is the better known version)
907. Tony Fox Sales
908. Real Cool World

909. Nile Rodgers
910. Full stretch
911. Angie Bowie
912. Jump They Say
913. Mark Romanek
914. Black Tie White Noise
915. Los Angeles and New York
916. Nile Rodgers
917. Nite Flights
918. a) The Wedding Song
   b) Miracle Goodnight
919. Mick Ronson
920. Mike Garson
921. Lester Bowie
922. Don't Let Me Down And Down
923. The Wedding
924. I Know It's Gunna Happen Someday
925. Mick Ronson
926. David Mallet
927. Al B. Sure!
928. MTV The Hits
929. Miracle Goodnight
930. Nirvana
931. The Video Collection
932. Freddie Burretti
933. Cyrinda Foxe
934. Wild Is The Wind
935. Mick Rock
936. Buddha Of Suburbia
937. All The Madmen
938. Lenny Kravitz
939. Ian Fish U.K. Heir

the 1990s

940. **The Singles Collection**
941. George Michael, K. D. Lang and Mick Hucknall
942. **Heaven And Hull**
943. *Like A Rolling Stone*
944. *All The Young Dudes* (the Freddie Mercury Tribute Concert version)
945. *Soul Love*
946. Iman
947. Laura Ashley
948. Mustique
949. *The Hearts Filthy Lesson*
950. Hartford
951. Zachory Alford
952. Nine Inch Nails
953. Morrissey
954. Reeves Gabrels
955. Gail Ann Dorsey
956. **1. Outside**
957. 19
958. *Strangers When We Meet*
959. a) *I'm Deranged*
    b) *Hallo Spaceboy*
960. Brian Eno
961. Oxford Town
962. Nathan Adler
963. David Bowie
964. Erdal Kizilcay
965. *The Hearts Filthy Lesson*
966. a) *Nathan Adler*
    b) *Ramona A. Stone*
    c) *Algeria Touchshriek*
967. **People From Bad Homes**

968. The Astronettes
969. Robert Sandall
970. Showgirls
971. The Man Who Sold The World
972. The Man Who Sold The World
973. Hallo Spaceboy, The Man Who Sold The World and *Strangers When We Meet*
974. The White Room
975. Under Pressure, The Voyeur Of Utter Destruction (As Beauty), Hallo Spaceboy and *Boys Keep Swinging*
976. Birmingham NEC
977. David Byrne
978. Madonna
979. John Peel
980. Outstanding Contribution To Music
981. Tony Blair
982. The Pet Shop Boys
983. Moonage Daydream and *Under Pressure*
984. Under Pressure and *Moonage Daydream*
985. Phoenix Festival
986. "Heroes"
987. Basquiat
988. Andy Warhol
989. Julian Schnabel
990. Gary Oldman
991. A Small Plot Of Land
992. Telling Lies
993. The Bridge School Benefit Concerts
994. Reeves Gabrels and Gail Ann Dorsey
995. Aladdin Sane
996. Neil Young and his wife Pegi
997. VH-1 Fashion Awards

998. George Tremlett
999. Madison Square Garden
1000. Frank Black (Pixies)
1001. Quicksand
1002. Lou Reed
1003. I'm Waiting For The Man, Dirty Boulevard and *White Light White Heat*
1004. Gail Ann Dorsey
1005. Billy Corgan
1006. Avi Lewis
1007. Floria Sigismondi
1008. Lost Highway
1009. Earthling
1010. USA (New York) and Switzerland (Montreux)
1011. Mark Plati
1012. Battle For Britain (The Letter)
1013. Heinrich Harrer
1014. a) I'm Afraid Of Americans
    b) The Last Thing You Should Do
1015. Law (Earthlings On Fire)
1016. a) Zachory Alford
1017. Alexander McQueen
1018. Gail Ann Dorsey
1019. Little Wonder
1020. Saturday Night Live
1021. David received the Hollywood Walk Of Fame Star
1022. Dead Man Walking
1023. The Deram Anthology 1966 – 1968
1024. Planet Of Dreams
1025. Germany
1026. Quicksand
1027. O Superman

1028. Gail Ann Dorsey
1029. The Phoenix Festival
1030. Tao Jones Index
1031. MTV Live From The 10 Spot
1032. Argentina
1033. Mother
1034. Seven Years In Tibet
1035. The *M.O.R.* track used the same chord progression as *Boys Keep Swinging* and *Fantastic Voyage*
1036. I'm Afraid Of Americans
1037. I Can't Read
1038. The GQ Men Of The Year Awards
1039. Always Crashing In The Same Car
1040. Perfect Day
1041. Lou Reed
1042. Hurt
1043. Earthling In The City
1044. Bowienet
1045. Sailor
1046. Mark Adams
1047. Eddie Izzard
1048. Velvet Goldmine
1049. Brian Slade
1050. Lindsay Kemp
1051. A Foggy Day (In London Town)
1052. (Safe In This) Sky Life
1053. Il Mio West
1054. Gunslingers Revenge' in the US (Sept 2005)
1055. Jack Sikora
1056. Giovanni Veronesi
1057. Placebo
1058. 20th Century Boy

1059. Everybody Loves Sunshine
1060. B.U.S.T.E.D.
1061. Bernie
1062. Berklee College Of Music
1063. Without You I'm Nothing
1064. Stigmata
1065. VH1 Storytellers
1066. Reeves Gabrels
1067. Can't Help Thinking About Me
1068. Holly Palmer and Lani Groves
1069. Thursday's Child
1070. Walter Stern
1071. The Hunger
1072. Terence Stamp
1073. Hours
1074. Reeves Gabrels
1075. a) New Angels Of Promise
   b) Something In The Air
1076. Eartha Kitt
1077. Alex Grant
1078. The Dreamers
1079. Tim was the photographer responsible for the cover's artwork
1080. Mike Levesque
1081. Bermuda
1082. If I'm Dreaming My Life
1083. Holly Palmer
1084. Mark Plati
1085. Netaid
1086. USA and Switzerland
1087. Survive and *The Pretty Things Are Going To Hell*
1088. Page Hamilton

ALL MY ~~IDIOT~~ 1500 QUESTIONS

1089. Emm Gryner and Holly Palmer
1090. TFI Friday
1091. Chris Evans
1092. Omikron: The Nomad Soul
1093. Boz
1094. Iman 1631
1095. Drive In Saturday
1096. Commandeur dans l'Ordre des Arts et des Lettres (Commander of Arts and Literature)
1097. LiveAndWell.com
1098. The 'Earthling' Tour of 1997
1099. Jeremy Paxman
1100. Later With Jools

the 1990s

Figure 15: Selection of 1990s' magazines and supplements from Author's Collection

ALL MY ~~IDIOT~~ 1500 QUESTIONS

the 2000s

Figure 16: Alamy Stock Photo

the 2000s
200 Questions

1101. Which English record producer remixed the track *Survive,* from the **Hours** album, for a single release in January 2000, on the Virgin record label?

1102. What was the name of the three-part documentary, presented by Mark Goodier, that was first broadcast on BBC Radio Two, in March 2000? The documentary looked at David's extraordinary career.

1103. The Canadian family feature film in which David appeared, 'Mr. Rice's Secret', was first shown at European festivals in the spring of 2000. By what other name was the film often known, having initially been a working title?
1104. Which character did David play?
1105. The film was based around a terminally ill boy called Owen. Who played the part of Owen?

1106. Which track from the **Hours** album did David contribute to the **American Psycho** soundtrack album, released in April 2000?

1107. In June 2000, David once more appeared on the Channel 4 TV music show, 'TFI Friday'. He performed four songs including *Absolute Beginners* and *Cracked Actor* but which two songs were actually broadcast?

1108. Which music festival did David headline in June 2000?

1109. On which famous stage did he perform?

1110. By way of introduction, which English folk song did pianist Mike Garson play solo, before David went on stage?

1111. With which song did David open his set?

1112. Which song from **Hunky Dory** did David perform, having also performed it at his only other Worthy Farm appearance, back in 1971?

1113. Who performed vocals with David on the track, *Under Pressure*?

1114. Who played drums?

1115. David recorded a set in June 2000, two days after Glastonbury, at the BBC Radio Theatre. Which song did he have to perform twice because he forgot the lyrics first time around?

1116. Which track from the **Low** album did David include in the set?

the 2000s

1117. Which Honour did David decline in the Queen's Birthday Honours of 2000?

1118. Which award did 'Bowienet' win, in July 2000? David personally accepted the award at the ceremony held at Studio 54 in New York.

1119. David also accepted an 'Online Pioneer Award', as well as performing which two songs, accompanied by Mike Garson?

1120. Which track from the **Hours** album was released as a single in July 2000 on the Virgin record label? CD1 of the single release included the original demo version as well as two remixes by Marius De Vries and Beck respectively.

1121. What is the name of David's daughter, born 15th August 2000?

1122. His daughter has two half siblings, name them.

1123. David was voted 'Most Stylish Man Of The Year', at which magazine's awards ceremony held in Covent Garden, in September 2000?

1124. The **Bowie At The Bccb** 3-CD set was released in September 2000 on the EMI record label. It became an instant collector's item when it was realised that one track on CD2, had been duplicated in error. Which track?

1125. The third CD in the set, was a bonus CD featuring much of the BBC Radio Theatre show recorded three months earlier. Which two 1960s tracks were

ALL MY ~~IDIOT~~ 1500 QUESTIONS

performed at the show, but were not included on the bonus CD?

1126. David made a surprise appearance at the 'VH1 Vogue Fashion Awards', in October 2000, to announce the winner of the 'Fashion Designer Of The Year Award'. Who won the award?
1127. Who presented the award to the winner?

1128. In a poll of fellow musicians in November 2000, which music publication voted David the most influential artist of all time?

1129. Which two of his own songs did David perform at 'The Tibet House Benefit Concert' at Carnegie Hall in New York, in February 2001?
1130. Who played bass guitar?

1131. In March 2001, David narrated a BBC TV Omnibus documentary about which English artist, born 1891 and died 1959?

1132. Intended to be released in March 2001, what was the name of David's lost album, ultimately shelved following a dispute with the record company? The album was predominantly re-recordings of songs from the early part of his career.
1133. Who co-produced the album with David?
1134. At Mark Plati's suggestion, which multi-instrumentalist from Indiana was hired to contribute overdubs on the album?

170

the 2000s

1135. Which family member died on the 2nd April 2001, at the nursing home in St. Albans where she lived?

1136. Which song did David contribute to the **A Knight's Tale** soundtrack album, released in May 2001?

1137. David contributed vocals to the **Moulin Rouge** soundtrack album, released in May 2001. Which song, first recorded by American jazz singer Nat King Cole, did he perform?

1138. Beck covered which of David's 1974 songs on the same album?

1139. Released on the Edel record label in June 2001, which Pete Townshend song did David contribute to the compilations album **Substitute – The Songs Of The Who**?

1140. In which film, first released in the US in September 2001, and starring Ben Stiller and Owen Wilson, did David make a cameo appearance as himself, judging a walk off between rival male models?

1141. David opened proceedings at 'The Concert For New York City', in October 2001 at Madison Square Garden, following the 9/11 attacks. Which two songs did he perform?

1142. Which celebrity appeared on the ITV show 'Popstars In Their Eyes', in October 2001, performing as David singing *Starman?* He won the competition.

ALL MY ~~IDIOT~~ 1500 QUESTIONS

1143. The compilation covers album **Diamond Gods – Interpretations Of Bowie** was released in November 2001, on the Invisible Hands Music record label. Two female artists each covered *Heroes*. One was Blondie, who was the other?
1144. Which track did Bad Manners frontman, Buster Bloodvessel, cover?

1145. Name David's two friends from the 1960s who together unveiled a plaque at The Three Tuns pub, home of the Beckenham Arts Lab, in December 2001.
1146. By what name was the pub known at the time of the unveiling?

1147. David performed at 'The Tibet House Benefit Concert' in February 2002, singing which two songs?
1148. The evening began with unknown artists, Chocolate Genius, performing an acoustic version of which of David's songs from 1972?

1149. Which track from David's **Tonight** album, was sampled on a new club track by New York producer, Scumfrog, in April 2002?

1150. In May 2002, David performed five songs at the first ever 'Tribeca Film Festival' in New York. As well as performing *China Girl*, *Let's Dance* and *I'm Afraid Of Americans* from older albums, he also performed which two new tracks from the upcoming new album?

1151. Name David's 22nd studio album, released in June 2002, on the ISO/Columbia record label.

the 2000s

1152. The first album since **Tin Machine** not to feature Reeves Gabrels, which Irish guitarist featured for the first time, and also became a regular member of the touring band?
1153. The cover, *Cactus,* was a song written and originally performed by which American alternative rock band?
1154. Tony Visconti was back in the fold, co-producing the album with David. Which of David's albums did Visconti last produce?
1155. On which track did The Who's Pete Townshend play a guitar solo?
1156. Who wrote the track, *I Took A Trip On A Gemini Spaceship?*
1157. Working with David for the first time, who designed the album cover?
1158. Solve the following anagrams to identify the two album tracks:-
    a)   *Your Audible Wolves*
    b)   *Arise Honey Yves*
1159. Which track was inspired by 'The Uncle Floyd Show', a US TV show first aired in the 1970s?
1160. Dave Grohl played guitar on which track written by Neil Young?
1161. Which member(s) of the 1983 'Serious Moonlight' world tour brass section, contributed saxophone to the album?

1162. Broadcast in the US, in June 2002, David appeared on a show in New York, where fans phoned in asking him to play specific songs. What was the name of the show?
1163. Famous friend Moby called in to request which song?

1164. Which American television and radio personality hosted the show?

1165. For which festival in June 2002, was David chosen to be Artistic Director?
1166. Where was the festival held?
1167. On the final night of the festival, David performed all tracks from two of his own albums. Which two?
1168. The first song in David's encore featured American rock band, The Dandy Warhols. Which Velvet Underground track did they perform together?

1169. Who was the young girl who appeared in the *Slow Burn* promotional music video, released in some countries as a single in June 2002? It was uploaded to the official DavidBowieVEVO Youtube Channel nearly a decade later in 2011.

1170. In July 2002, the BBC broadcast a 45 minute TV interview special with Jonathan Ross. As well as performing *Fashion* and *Ziggy Stardust*, which two new songs from the **Heathen** album did David also perform?

1171. At which festival in Switzerland did David perform, in July 2002?
1172. With which song from the **Heathen** album did he open his set?
1173. David appeared for a second encore to perform all tracks, except one, from which album?
1174. Which was the one track from the album, not performed?

the 2000s

1175. Which book was published in July 2002, having been co-written by David himself and Mick Rock? David provided the text, Mick Rock the photos.

1176. In September 2002, which annual music prize for 'Best Album', listed David's album, **Heathen**, among its nominees?
1177. David didn't win, who did?
1178. David did not attend the ceremony, instead a video of him was shown on the big screen, performing which song from the **Heathen** album?
1179. All shortlisted nominees received an 'Album of the Year' trophy. Who accepted David's on his behalf?
1180. A Mercury Prize Compilation CD is released each year featuring one track from each nominee. Which of David's tracks from the **Heathen** album appeared on the CD?

1181. At which BBC studios in West London did David perform and record an exclusive concert for Radio Two, in September 2002?
1182. Who introduced the show?
1183. Which song, by David's own recollections, did he play live for the first time ever, conveying to the audience that "there are more words in this than War and Peace"?
1184. Which track from **Lodger** did he perform during the show?

1185. *Everyone Says 'Hi'* was a single released on the ISO/Columbia record label, in September 2002. One of the backup tracks was a previously mentioned track that David had written for the Rugrats Movie project back in 1998. To what name had the track been re-titled for this release?

1186. On whose BBC TV chat show did David appear, in September 2002?
1187. As well as being interviewed, which two songs did David perform?
1188. Which American actor was the only other guest on the show?

1189. David appeared once more on the 'Later With Jools' show, broadcast by the BBC in October 2002. He sang *5.15 The Angels Have Gone* and *Heathen (The Rays)*, both from the **Heathen** album, but which song from his back catalogue was also performed and broadcast?

1190. Wearing a blue silk suit, David performed *Rebel Rebel* and *Cactus* at which Radio City Music Hall, New York awards ceremony, in October 2002?

1191. What was the title of the Greatest Hits 2-DVD set containing forty seven music videos, released in October 2002 by EMI?
1192. Which three music videos from the 1980s were the censored versions of the originals?
1193. Which video was taken from the **Ziggy Stardust: The Motion Picture** film?

the 2000s

1194. The DVD1 Easter Eggs, included an alternate take of which track recorded for the 'Old Grey Whistle Test' in 1972?

1195. Which music video, directed by Stanley Dorfman, showed David playing guitar against a plain white background, in a style similar to that of the *Life On Mars?* music video?

1196. Which 1997 music video on DVD2, shot in New York, was directed by Dom & Nic?

1197. Which music video was the last on DVD2? A live version of the same track from a 1999 concert in Montmartre, Paris, was also included in the DVD2 Easter Eggs.

1198. Broadcast on VH1 in November 2002, who interviewed David and presented the show entitled 'VH1 Reveals'?

1199. Lou Reed's album **The Raven** was released in January 2003, on the Sire record label. For which track on the album did David contribute vocals?

1200. Which Royal Honour did David decline in 2003?

1201. What was the name of the 64 acre mountain area that David bought in 2003, building a house almost identical to the one he had built on the Caribbean island of Mustique back in the 1980s?

1202. David attended his third 'Tibet House Benefit Concert', in February 2003. As well as performing

Loving The Alien and *Heathen (The Rays)*, on which song did he perform a duet with Ray Davies?

1203. Broadcast on BBC Three, what was the title of the documentary series that examined the finances of prominent figures? David was the subject of one such documentary, broadcast in March 2003.

1204. Released in April 2003, which track did David contribute to the Warchild album, **Hope**?

1205. Who appeared on the May 2003 front cover of British 'Vogue' magazine, complete with the **Aladdin Sane** album cover lightning bolt flash?

1206. Which award did David win, in May 2003, for his contribution (narration) to the 2002 film 'Hollywood Rocks the Movies: The 1970s'?

1207. David appeared in a French TV commercial for Vittel Water, in June 2003. Which new song was used for the commercial's backing track?

1208. Who was the 'lookalike' who appeared in the commercial alongside David?

1209. *Bring Me The Disco King* appeared on the soundtrack album of which film, released in September 2003?

1210. Recorded and broadcast in September 2003 on the French TV show 'Trafic Musique', on which song did David duet with Damon Albarn?

1211. At which London Hammersmith studios did David premiere the upcoming new album, in September 2003, playing all tracks live and streaming it via satellite to a number of cinemas around the world?
1212. Which song from the **Low** album did David perform prior to playing the upcoming new album in full?
1213. At the conclusion of the new album set, a questions and answers session was hosted, by whom?
1214. Another seven tracks from the back catalogue were then played to round off the evening. Which one song from the **The Rise and Fall of Ziggy Stardust and the Spiders from Mars** album did David choose to play?

1215. David appeared on the Jonathan Ross show once more, broadcast in September 2003. As well as being interviewed, which two songs did he perform?

1216. Name David's 23rd studio album, released in September 2003, on the ISO/Columbia record label.
1217. In which New York studios was the album recorded and produced?
1218. Which track was written by Jonathan Richman and recorded by The Modern Lovers on their self-titled debut album in 1976.
1219. Solve the following anagrams to identify the two album tracks:-
    a) *Gutsy Eileen Holt*
    b) *Overt Legend*
1220. The digipak release of the album included a second CD, featuring three tracks only. One track was a revamped *Rebel Rebel,* what were the other two?

ALL MY ~~IDIOT~~ 1500 QUESTIONS

1221. Who wrote the track *Try Some Buy Some*?
1222. Which track ends the original standard release of the album, and at 7 minutes 45 seconds, is also the longest track on the album? It had first been recorded for both the **Black Tie White Noise** and **Earthling** albums, but was ultimately not included on either.
1223. Which of these musicians played guitar on the album?
    a) David Bowie
    b) Gerry Leonard
    c) Mark Plati
    d) Earl Slick
1224. The tour edition of the album included which bonus track?
1225. According to David himself, which track did he write after reading an article about Kellogg Brown & Root?
1226. Which American Jazz singer provided backing vocals on the album?

1227. *New Killer Star* was released as a DVD single in September 2003, on the ISO/Columbia record label. Which Sigue Sigue Sputnik track did David cover as part of the release?
1228. The new wave band had themselves covered which of David's 1974 songs on their 1990 album, **The First Generation**?

1229. At which awards ceremony, in October 2003 at the Royal Albert Hall, did hosts Elizabeth Hurley and Denis Leary, introduce a specially recorded video of David performing *Fashion*?

1230. In which European country did the 'Reality' Worldwide Concert Tour get under way, in October 2003?

1231. As well as playing guitar in the band, who was Music Director for the tour?

1232. In which French city, was a show cancelled in November 2003, due to David suffering from laryngitis?

1233. In May 2004, what was the name of the lighting engineer who sadly fell to his death prior to the show, in Miami, Florida?

1234. Which was the only song from the **Young Americans** album, to regularly feature in the setlist?

1235. Which of these musicians was NOT a member of the touring band?
      a) Earl Slick
      b) Mike Garson
      c) Zachary Alford
      d) Catherine Russell

1236. In which European capital was David hit in the eye with a lollipop whilst on stage?

1237. At which festival at the Seaclose Park in Newport, did David headline, in June 2004?

1238. David had the unenviable task of performing at the Newport festival, immediately following a 2-1 England defeat in the Euro 2004 Football Tournament, to which nation?

1239. At which European festival, in June 2004, did David perform for the most part in some discomfort, before being taken to hospital where a blocked artery was diagnosed? This turned out to be the last show of the tour, as remaining shows were cancelled.

ALL MY ~~IDIOT~~ 1500 QUESTIONS

1240. Which festival had David been due to headline in Scotland, just two weeks later?

1241. Released in November 2003 on the Zona record label, David provided vocals on the track entitled *Saviour*, on the album **Breasticles**. Name the artist who had herself previously contributed vocals to David's **Heathen** album in 2002.

1242. On whose BBC TV chat show did David appear, for a second time, in November 2003?

1243. As well as being interviewed, which two songs did David perform?

1244. Who were the other two guests on the show?

1245. The December issue of **Q** Magazine, included a free CD album entitled **Best Of 03**. Containing 18 tracks from the year, which of David's songs was included?

1246. For which Earl Slick album, released in December 2003 on the Sanctuary record label, did David contribute vocals on the track, *Isn't It Evening (The Revolutionary)*?

1247. Which rock photographer's work with David was displayed in London's Proud Gallery Camden Moss, for a six week run starting February 2004? The exhibition was entitled 'Bowie: 78-90'.

1248. Released in March 2004, which track recorded by David appeared on the compilation album, **Next – A Tribute To Jacques Brel**?

the 2000s

1249. With whom did David duet, contributing a track to the **Shrek 2** soundtrack album, released in May 2004?
1250. Which song from **Hunky Dory** did they contribute?

1251. Which Radio Two DJ had a show called 'Drivetime', on which David appeared in June 2004 to promote his new single, the mash-up *Rebel Never Gets Old?*
1252. Who produced the mash-up?

1253. A live DVD of the 'Reality' world tour was released in October 2004. What was the title of the DVD?
1254. The concert footage was culled from two nights in November 2003, at which venue?
1255. With which 1974 song did David open the show?
1256. Which song was the very last to be played?
1257. Which one of these albums was not represented in the DVD's track listing?
    a) The Man Who Sold The World
    b) Aladdin Sane
    c) Lodger
    d) Tonight

1258. Which Canadian songwriter and producer released an album, in November 2004, entitled **Loving The Alien**? It featured cover versions of eleven of David's songs.

1259. Which track by David featured on the 2-CD set **UK Music Hall Of Fame**, released in November 2004?

1260. Moby released an album entitled **Hotel,** in March 2005. Which track was a tribute to David?

1261. The American military science fiction film, 'Stealth', was released in July 2005. Which new track did David contribute to its soundtrack album, released the same month on the Epic record label?

1262. David appeared at the 'Fashion Rocks Awards' ceremony in New York, in September 2005, performing *Life On Mars?* backed by Mike Garson on piano. With which Canadian indie rock band did David then perform two more tracks?

1263. Which of his own songs did David and the band perform together?

1264. Which of the band's songs did they then perform together?

1265. Whose book, launched in the autumn of 2005, was entitled 'The Beauty Of Colour'?

1266. Which BBC One TV series starring John Simm and Philip Glenister started broadcasting in January 2006? The title was a reference to one of David's songs.

1267. In January 2006, Joan As Police Woman released the single *My Gurl* on the Reveal record label. Which of David's songs from the **Diamond Dogs** album did she cover on the B side?

1268. At which awards ceremony, in Los Angeles, did David receive a 'Recording Academy Lifetime Achievement Award', in February 2006?

1269. On whose show at the Royal Albert Hall, in May 2006, did David make a special guest appearance?

1270. Which two songs did David perform?

1271. Released in May 2006, David performed backing vocals on a single entitled *Province*. Taken from their album **Return To Cookie Mountain**, what is the name of the band with whom David collaborated?

1272. Broadcast in September 2006, on which BBC TV show, written by Ricky Gervais and Stephen Merchant, did David appear as himself?

1273. What was the name of Ricky Gervais' character?

1274. Ricky's character is the main star of which fictitious TV sitcom?

1275. Which Scottish actress played the part of Gervais' friend, Maggie Jacobs?

1276. In what turned out to be his last recognised public performance, David appeared at 'The Black Ball' fundraiser event for 'Keep A Child Alive' in November 2006. With whom did he perform a duet?

1277. Which of David's songs did they sing together?

1278. Which two other songs did David perform?

1279. Released in November 2006, and directed by Christopher Nolan, David appeared in which film about two rival stage magicians in London?

ALL MY ~~IDIOT~~ 1500 QUESTIONS

1280. Who played the part of the magician, Robert Angier?
1281. Who played the part of the magician, Alfred Borden?
1282. Which character did David play?

1283. Premiered in France in November 2006, for which fantasy animation film did David voice the character, Emperor Maltazard?
1284. Other celebrities also voiced characters for the project. Which one of the following artists didn't?
    a)   Madonna
    b)   Michael Caine
    c)   Robert De Niro
    d)   Snoop Dogg

1285. Which festival that took place in New York, in May 2007, was David chosen to curate?
1286. In what was his last appearance on a stage, which artist did David introduce by singing a few lines of *chubby little loser*?

1287. Published in a limited edition of only 2000 copies, and signed by both himself and David, whose book was released in 2007 by Genesis Publications?
1288. The book itself was the untold story of three years writing, recording, performing, living and travelling with David. What was the title of the book?

1289. At which awards ceremony in New York, did David receive a 'Lifetime Achievement Award', in June 2007?

the 2000s

1290. In June 2007, EMI released a DVD version of the Glass Spider VHS tape, which itself had been culled from shows in Sydney in 1987 and released a year later. The DVD release also included a 2-CD audio recording of a Glass Spider concert from which North American city?

1291. For which American animated TV series, broadcast in November 2007, did David lend his voice?
1292. What was the name of the episode featuring David?
1293. Which character did David voice?

1294. Premiered at the 'Sundown Film Festival' in Utah, in January 2008, which character did David play in the film, 'August'?

1295. Which BBC One TV series starring Philip Glenister and Keeley Hawes, started broadcasting in February 2008? The series was a sequel to that in Q1266 and its title was once again a reference to another of David's songs.

1296. In May 2008, David contributed vocals to two tracks, namely *Falling Down* and *Fannin' Street*, on an album entitled **Anywhere I Lay My Head**. Who was the artist?

1297. **Iselect** (or **Iselectbowie**) was a collection of David's songs, released on a CD album on the EMI record label that was exclusively available as a free gift in June 2008, with which British newspaper?

ALL MY ~~IDIOT~~ 1500 QUESTIONS

1298. Found predominantly in Malaysia, Singapore and Indonesia in 2008, what was the name of the orange haired spider named in honour of David?

1299. David's son Duncan directed his debut film during 2008 and saw it first premiered at the 'Sundown Film Festival' in January 2009. Name the film.

1300. In an American comedy drama film directed by Todd Graff, and released in August 2009 in the US, Will Burton was a music enthusiast and a David Bowie fan. He sent e-mails to David every day, although he never got a reply. David made a brief cameo appearance at the end of the film. Name the film.

Figure 17: Selection of items from Author's Collection, featuring works or releases from the 2000s

the 2000s
200 Answers

1101. Marius De Vries
1102. Golden Years – The David Bowie Story
1103. Exhuming Mr. Rice
1104. William Rice
1105. Bill Switzer
1106. Something In The Air (American Psycho Remix)
1107. *Wild Is The Wind* and *Starman*
1108. Glastonbury
1109. Pyramid Stage
1110. Greensleeves
1111. Wild Is The Wind
1112. Changes
1113. Gail Ann Dorsey
1114. Sterling Campbell
1115. Ziggy Stardust
1116. Always Crashing In The Same Car
1117. CBE
1118. Yahoo! Internet Award for 'Best Artist Site'

1119. Wild Is The Wind and *Life On Mars?*

1120. Seven

1121. Alexandria Zahra Jones

1122. Duncan (David & Angie) and Zulekha Haywood (Iman & ex-pro basketball player, Spencer Haywood)

1123. GQ magazine's Men Of The Year Awards

1124. Ziggy Stardust

1125. The London Boys and *I Dig Everything*

1126. Stella McCartney

1127. Paul McCartney

1128. NME

1129. Heroes and *Silly Boy Blue*

1130. Tony Visconti

1131. Stanley Spencer

1132. Toy

1133. Mark Plati

1134. Lisa Germano

1135. David's mother, Margaret Mary Jones (Peggy)

1136. Golden Years

1137. Nature Boy

1138. Diamond Dogs

1139. Pictures Of Lily

1140. Zoolander

1141. America (Simon & Garfunkel) and *Heroes*

1142. Boy George

1143. Nico

1144. The Laughing Gnome

1145. Mary Finnigan and Christina Ostrom

1146. The Rat and Parrot

1147. I Would Be Your Slave and *Space Oddity*

1148. Soul Love

1149. Loving The Alien

1150. Slow Burn and *Afraid*
1151. Heathen
1152. Gerry Leonard
1153. Pixies
1154. Scary Monsters (And Super Creeps)
1155. Slow Burn
1156. The Legendary Stardust Cowboy
1157. Jonathan Barnbrook
1158. a) I Would Be Your Slave
  b) Everyone Says 'Hi'
1159. Slip Away
1160. I've Been Waiting For You
1161. All three of them did; Lenny Pickett, Stan Harrison and Steve Elson
1162. A&E Live By Request
1163. Sound And Vision
1164. Mark McEwen
1165. Meltdown Festival
1166. Southbank Centre – including The Royal Festival Hall, The Queen Elizabeth Hall and The Haywood Gallery
1167. Low followed by **Heathen**
1168. White Light White Heat
1169. Hayley Nicholas
1170. Slip Away and *Everyone Says 'Hi'*
1171. Montreux Jazz Festival
1172. Sunday
1173. Low
1174. Weeping Wall
1175. Moonage Daydream, The Life And Times Of Ziggy Stardust
1176. Panasonic Mercury Music Prize

1177. Ms. Dynamite (**A little Deeper**)
1178. Everyone Says 'Hi'
1179. Jools Holland
1180. Slow Burn
1181. Maida Vale Studios
1182. Jonathan Ross
1183. The Bewlay Brothers
1184. Look Back In Anger
1185. Safe
1186. Parkinson
1187. Everyone Says 'Hi' and *Life On Mars?*
1188. Tom Hanks
1189. Rebel Rebel
1190. VH1 Vogue Fashion Awards
1191. Best Of Bowie
1192. China Girl, Loving The Alien and *Day-In Day-Out*
1193. Ziggy Stardust
1194. Oh You Pretty Things
1195. Be My Wife
1196. I'm Afraid Of Americans
1197. Survive
1198. Gary Crowley
1199. Hop Frog
1200. A Knighthood
1201. Little Tonshi Mountain, located in the Catskill mountains
1202. Waterloo Sunset
1203. Liquid Assets
1204. Metro remix of *Everyone Says 'Hi'*
1205. Kate Moss
1206. Daytime Emmy Award
1207. Never Get Old

1208. David Brighton
1209. Underworld
1210. Fashion
1211. The Riverside Studios
1212. A New Career In A New Town
1213. Jonathan Ross
1214. Hang On To Yourself
1215. New Killer Star and *Modern Love*
1216. Reality
1217. The Looking Glass Studios
1218. Pablo Picasso
1219. a) The Loneliest Guy
   b) Never Get Old
1220. Fly and *Queen Of All The Tarts*
1221. George Harrison
1222. Bring Me The Disco King
1223. They all played guitar
1224. *Waterloo Sunset*
1225. Fall Dog Bombs The Moon
1226. Catherine Russell
1227. Love Missile F1-11
1228. Rebel Rebel
1229. Fashion Rocks Awards
1230. Denmark
1231. Gerry Leonard
1232. Toulouse (Le Zenith)
1233. Walter Thomas
1234. Fame
1235. c) Zachary Alford wasn't
1236. Oslo
1237. Isle Of Wight Festival
1238. France

1239. The Hurricane Festival in Scheessel, Germany
1240. T in the Park
1241. Kristeen Young
1242. Parkinson
1243. The Loneliest Guy and Ziggy Stardust
1244. Clive James and Victoria Beckham
1245. Fall Dog Bombs The Moon
1246. Zig Zag
1247. Denis O'Regan
1248. Amsterdam
1249. Butterfly Boucher
1250. Changes
1251. Johnny Walker
1252. Mark Vidler
1253. A Reality Tour
1254. The Point, Dublin, Ireland
1255. Rebel Rebel
1256. Ziggy Stardust
1257. **b) Aladdin Sane** wasn't
1258. Danny Michel
1259. Life On Mars?
1260. Spiders
1261. (She Can) Do That
1262. Arcade Fire
1263. Five Years
1264. Wake Up
1265. Iman
1266. Life On Mars
1267. Sweet Thing
1268. The 48th Grammy Awards
1269. Dave Gilmour
1270. Arnold Layne and Comfortably Numb

1271. TV On The Radio
1272. Extras
1273. Andy Millman
1274. When The Whistle Blows
1275. Ashley Jensen
1276. Alicia Keys
1277. *Changes*
1278. *Wild Is The Wind* and *Fantastic Voyage*
1279. The Prestige
1280. Hugh Jackman
1281. Christian Bale
1282. Nikola Tesla
1283. Arthur and the Invisibles (Arthur and the Minimoys)
1284. b) Michael Caine didn't
1285. The High Line Festival
1286. Ricky Gervais
1287. Geoff MacCormack
1288. From Station To Station, Travels with Bowie, 1973-1976
1289. The Webby Awards
1290. Montreal
1291. Spongebob Squarepants
1292. Spongebob's Atlantis Squarepantis
1293. Lord Royal Highness
1294. Cyrus Ogilvie
1295. Ashes To Ashes
1296. American actress, Scarlett Johansson
1297. The Mail On Sunday
1298. Heteropoda Davidbowie
1299. Moon
1300. Bandslam

ALL MY ~~IDIOT~~ 1500 QUESTIONS

the 2010s

Figure 18: Author's photos

the 2010s
200 Questions

1301. A 2-CD album, **A Reality Tour**, was released in January 2010 on the ISO/Columbia record label. The track listing was essentially the same as the DVD released back in 2004, but which three additional bonus tracks had been added at the end?

1302. Which 2-CD compilation album, released in January 2010 on the Deram record label, featured both mono and stereo versions of tracks, single mixes, unreleased tracks and alternate takes, as well as the BBC Radio One 'Top Gear' session from December 1967?

1303. **We Were So Turned On** was the title of a covers album released in September 2010, featuring various artists performing some of David's songs. It included a version of *Boys Keep Swinging* by Duran Duran as well as a version of which song by Carla Bruni, the wife of the then French president, Nicolas Sarkozy?

1304. 'Special' and 'Deluxe' box set editions of the **Station To Station** album were released in September 2010. Which previously unreleased, but heavily bootlegged and much sought after 1976 live concert, was included in each edition?

1305. Which book, written by Kevin Cann and often referred to as The Bowie Bible, was first published in November 2010 and provides an in-depth visual chronology of David's early life and career in London?

1306. Which of David's songs did the X-Factor finalists cover in November 2010, in aid of the 'Help For Heroes' charity? Unsurprisingly, it reached No. 1 in the UK charts.

1307. Premiered in February 2011, a TV commercial for which motor car featured a snippet of *Space Oddity* and a Ziggy tattoo, as well as Thierry Henry, Rihanna and burlesque dancer Dita Von Teese?

1308. First aired in February 2011 at the Super Bowl, a commercial for BMW Diesel Engines featured which of David's songs from the early 1970s?

1309. Described as a science fiction action thriller film, and premiered in March 2011 at South by Southwest, what was the second film to be directed by Duncan Jones?

the 2010s

1310. The New York Dolls opened their short UK tour in March 2011, at the O2 Newcastle Academy. Which of David's regular band members had joined them as guitarist for the tour?

1311. Whose album, released in July 2011, was entitled **The Bowie Variations for Piano**?

1312. In August 2011, Canadian artist Andrew Kolb created an illustrated children's book based entirely on which of David's songs? He ultimately hit legal red tape and had to remove the book due to copyright infringement.

1313. Which artist released a 42 track anthology of his life's work in October 2011, on the Cherry Red record label, entitled **For Sarah, Raquel and David**?

1314. We know David was a fan, but to whom did the names Sarah and Raquel refer? Both were fans too.

1315. In December 2011, retired BBC cameraman John Henshall, found a long lost 'Top Of The Pops' clip of David and the Spiders, from 1973, performing which song?

1316. Which two of David's albums did Radio Two DJ Johnnie Walker review for his 'Long Players' show in February 2012?

1317. In the presence of both Mick 'Woody' Woodmansey and Trevor Bolder, who in March 2012, unveiled the blue plaque to Ziggy Stardust on the wall of 23

ALL MY ~~IDIOT~~ 1500 QUESTIONS

Heddon Street in London, where the black and white photos for the album cover had been taken?

1318. Which of David's singles celebrated a 40th anniversary limited edition 7" picture disc release, as part of Record Store Day, April 2012?

1319. What was the title of the book, a collaboration between David and Masayoshi Sukita, that was published by Genesis Publications, in April 2012?

1320. Which of David's ex-record producers published a book in June 2012, entitled 'Abbey Road To Ziggy Stardust'?

1321. In June 2012, BBC Four aired a documentary entitled 'David Bowie & The Story Of Ziggy Stardust'. Who narrated it?

1322. Which filmmaker travelled to New York to try, unsuccessfully as it turned out, to persuade David to participate in the July 2012 London Olympic Games Opening Ceremony?

1323. Which of David's songs was played during Great Britain's entrance at the Games' Opening Ceremony?

1324. The ICA celebrated David's work in film with a three day festival in London, starting in August 2012. What was the name of the festival?

1325. Which Irish University hosted 'Strange Fascination?', a Symposium on David Bowie, in October 2012?

the 2010s

1326. Who did David's son, Duncan, marry in November 2012?

1327. Without any prior warning or fanfare, which new song was released as a single by David, on the ISO/Columbia record label, on his 66th birthday in January 2013?
1328. Who directed the accompanying music video for the single?
1329. Name the female whose 'face in the hole' puppet appeared in the music video alongside David's.
1330. What wording was on the T-shirt worn by David towards the end of the music video, a reference to Hermione Farthingale, his girlfriend from the late 1960s?

1331. *The Stars (Are Out Tonight)* was the next single to be taken from the upcoming new album, and was released in February 2013 on the ISO/Columbia record label. Who directed the accompanying music video, having previously worked with David on the *Little Wonder* music video of 1997?
1332. Who played the part of David's wife in the music video?

1333. Name David's 24th studio album, released in March 2013, on the ISO/Columbia record label.
1334. Recorded in secrecy over a two year period, who was the long-term engineer who worked on the album alongside David and Tony Visconti?

201

ALL MY ~~IDIOT~~ 1500 QUESTIONS

1335. Designed by Jonathan Barnbrook, the album cover was an adapted version of which one of David's earlier album covers, from the 1970s?
1336. The outro of which track slightly varied the drum pattern of the *Five Years* track from 1972?
1337. Who sang vocals with David on the track, *If You Can See Me?*
1338. Which of the following musicians did not feature on the album?
    a) Zachary Alford
    b) Steve Elson
    c) Robert Fripp
    d) David Torn
1339. Solve the following anagrams to identify the two album tracks:-
    a) *Accusation Pending*
    b) *Elvis Loots*
1340. The album reached No. 1 in the UK Albums Chart, the first to do so since which previous album?
1341. Which track was co-written by Gerry Leonard?
1342. On which track about a high school shooter did Earl Slick play lead guitar?
1343. Which track closed the album?

1344. At which museum in London did the 'David Bowie Is' exhibition open, in March 2013?
1345. The first costume to be seen in the exhibition was the Tokyo Pop black vinyl suit with white stripes. Who designed it?
1346. Which two co-curators wrote/compiled the 'David Bowie Is' book that accompanied the exhibition?

the 2010s

1347. In an elaborate April Fool's Day spoof in 2013, and with the help of Gerry Leonard, Ireland's national public service media broadcaster RTE, reported that David would be representing which country in the Eurovision Song Contest?

1348. Which Australian comedian and musician presented a three part documentary about David's career, for Absolute Radio in April 2013?

1349. Which track celebrated its 40th anniversary with the release of a 7" picture disc, as part of Record Store Day, April 2013?

1350. Name the Canadian astronaut who in May 2013, while rotating around the earth, recorded his own version of *Space Oddity*.

1351. In what turned out to be a trilogy of documentary films for the BBC, what was the title of the first of these films, released in May 2013, covering five key years in David's career?

1352. Who directed this, and the remaining two documentaries?

1353. Name the Australian street artist who, in June 2013, painted the Aladdin Sane mural on the wall of Morley's department store, opposite the Brixton Tube Station.

ALL MY ~~IDIOT~~ 1500 QUESTIONS

1354. What was the connection, in June 2013, between David, H.R. Giger, Judith Merril, Joanna Russ and J.R.R.Tolkein?

1355. In June 2013, how did the NHS use David's iconic **Aladdin Sane** album cover shot, as inspiration for a new campaign? The accompanying slogan read, 'You can be heroes, for more than one day'.

1356. In June 2013, which track from the latest album was released as a single on white square shaped vinyl, on the ISO/Columbia record label?

1357. The fourth single from the **The Next Day** album, *Valentine's Day*, was released in August 2013 on the ISO/Columbia record label. Which non album track was on the B side?

1358. On which Arcade Fire single did David contribute vocals, released in September 2013 on the Merge record label?

1359. Released on a limited edition 12" vinyl, to which fictional band was the single credited?

1360. Released in September 2013, 'Rush' was a film centred around ex-racing drivers, James Hunt and Niki Lauda. Which of David's songs appeared on the soundtrack album?

1361. In October 2013, BBC6 Music aired for the first time, a long lost 15 minute tape of David talking in 1973 about some of the tracks on his **Pin Ups** album. The

the 2010s

tape simply had 'Radio Show' written on it and had been made by David and Ken Scott. Who unearthed the rare find?

1362. In whose 'L'invitation Au Voyage' advertising campaign did David appear in November 2013?
1363. Which song from **The Next Day** album did David sing in the commercial?

1364. **The Next Day Extra** was a 3-disc collector's edition of the original album, and was released in November 2013. One of the discs was a DVD containing which four promotional music videos?
1365. Which track from the album, albeit the *Hello Steve Reich Mix*, was released as a promotional single to coincide with the release of the collector's edition?

1366. In February 2014, at the 34th 'Brit Awards' in London, David became the oldest artist to win which award?
1367. James Corden was compere for the evening but who introduced and presented David's award?
1368. Who, wearing David's 'Woodland Creatures' jumpsuit from the Ziggy Stardust days, collected the award on his behalf?

1369. David released a new compilation album, **Nothing Has Changed**, in November 2014, on the Parlophone record label. As well as different mixes, versions and edits of well known songs, which brand new song featuring the Maria Schneider Orchestra, was also included on the album?

1370. The title **Nothing Has Changed** was taken from a lyric, from which track on the **Heathen** album?
1371. Which track, originally entitled *Toy* and recorded during the unreleased **Toy** album sessions of 2000, had been re-titled by the time of its inclusion on the compilation album?
1372. Which track, originally written and recorded in 1971, and then re-recorded during the **Toy** sessions of 2000, also appeared on the compilation album?

1373. *Sue (Or In A Season Of Crime)* was released as a single in November 2014, on the Parlophone record label. Which new track was recorded for the B side?

1374. In December 2014 on a celebrity edition of the BBC One TV show, 'Mastermind', which journalist, presenter and political editor chose 'David Bowie 1966 to 1976' as his specialist subject?

1375. In June 2015, Holy Holy, the supergroup put together by Mick 'Woody' Woodmansey and Tony Visconti, released a live album of their September 2014 gig at which London venue?
1376. Which of David's albums did they perform in its entirety before embarking on a set of songs from his back catalogue?
1377. Guest singers performed at the gig, but which Heaven 17 singer regularly fronted the band?

1378. In September 2015, Parlophone released the first in a series of box sets containing albums, singles, B sides and other edits from David's career. The first set

the 2010s

covered the years from 1969 to 1973. What title was given to the box set?

1379. As well as the studio albums **David Bowie (Space Oddity)** through to **Pin Ups**, which two live albums also featured in the set?

1380. Which new track did David contribute to the Sky Atlantic TV show, 'The Last Panthers', in October 2015?

1381. Which track from the upcoming new album, was released as the lead single in November 2015, on the ISO/Columbia record label?
1382. Who directed the accompanying music video?
1383. Which French actress appeared in the music video, with a tail?

1384. In November 2015, a new species of butterfly was discovered, predominantly in Southern Cameroon. It was named 'Bicyclus Sigiussidorum' in honour of which of David's iconic characters?

1385. David made his last public appearance, in December 2015, at the premiere of his musical play at The New York Theatre Workshop. Name the musical play.
1386. Who co-wrote the musical with David?
1387. Who directed the musical?
1388. The musical was based on the book by Walter Tevis which in 1976 became the film that gave David his first major acting role, as the character Thomas Jerome Newton, in 'The Man Who Fell To Earth'.

207

Who played Thomas Jerome Newton in the stage musical?

1389. Which track from the upcoming new album was released as a digital download single, in December 2015? It proved to be the last single released during David's lifetime.
1390. On whose BBC6 Music show, did the single receive its world premiere on the day of its release?
1391. On which celebrity UK Channel 5 TV show, did Angie Bowie appear at the start of January 2016?
1392. Name David's 25th studio album, released in January 2016, on the ISO/Columbia record label.
1393. Which two tracks, previously recorded and released in 2014, were re-recorded for the album?
1394. Which track talked of the English Evergreens and was the only track not to have been demoed prior to going into the studios to record?
1395. Which American jazz musician played saxophone on the album?
1396. Who designed the album cover?
1397. Which instrument did Jason Lindner play?
1398. Who played bass guitar on the album?
1399. Solve the following anagrams to identify the two album tracks:-
   a) *Crab Talks*
   b) *Remove Gills*
1400. On which track did David play a harmonica solo, similar to the one he performed on *A New Career In A New Town,* back in 1977?

the 2010s

1401. Who played drums on the album?
1402. Which track is notable for its inclusion of Nadsat, a fictional language created by Anthony Burgess for his novel 'A Clockwork Orange'?

1403. On what date did David die, losing an 18 month battle with liver cancer?
1404. Which drummer, who had worked with David in 1973-74, was celebrating his 70th birthday the same day David died?
1405. The news of David's passing broke in the UK around 7:00am on Monday 11th January 2016, and tributes and specially arranged programmes dominated the media that day. What was the name of the 30 minute documentary that BBC One aired that same evening?
1406. Channel 4 also aired a 45 minute documentary that night. What was it called?
1407. Both Bruce Springsteen and Madonna were touring at the time. In tribute to David, which one of his hits from the 1970s did they each perform their own version of, in concert?
1408. Who performed a moving tribute to David on Simon Mayo's 'Drivetime' BBC Two radio show, playing a piano rendition of *Life On Mars?* ?
1409. Melissa Etheridge was on a solo tour and she too performed one of David's songs in tribute. Which song?
1410. During the recording of a two hour TV special in Los Angeles, Elton John performed an extended piano version of which of David's songs?

1411. To whom had David sent a 'goodbye' email a few days earlier, saying "Thank You for the good times, they will never rot", and then signed off as "Dawn"?
1412. Having bought the property more than fifteen years earlier, where was David living at the time of his passing?

1413. In February 2016, Rick Wakeman recorded and released a CD in aid of Macmillan Cancer Support. Which two of David's songs did he perform on the CD?

1414. Which German luxury car manufacturer released a moon based commercial, in February 2016, to the soundtrack of David's *Starman?*

1415. At the annual pre-'Grammy Awards' show held in February 2016, American musician Beck, teamed up with the remaining members of Nirvana, as well as Dave Grohl, to perform which of David's classics?
1416. At the same party, Adam Lambert and Jack Antonoff ended the night with a performance of which of David's 1983 tracks?
1417. At the 58th 'Grammy Awards' ceremony itself in Los Angeles, Stefani Joanne Angelina Germanotta paid tribute to David, performing a medley of his songs. By what name is Stefani better known?

1418. At the 36th 'Brit Awards' held in London, in February 2016, David was posthumously awarded which award?
1419. Who gave a speech and presented the award?

the 2010s

1420. Which of David's close friends accepted the award and also gave a speech?
1421. David's regular band members then performed a two minute medley of some of his more popular tunes. Name the six band members.
1422. Who then joined the band on stage, to perform a stunning version of *Life On Mars?*?

1423. In April 2016, which track became the last track from the **Blackstar** album to be released as a single on the ISO/Columbia record label?
1424. Who designed and created the accompanying simplistic text based music video?

1425. Which sideman from Brooklyn toured the **Station To Station** album in the UK, in April 2016, performing all tracks in order, before then performing a collection of David's more popular career spanning songs?
1426. Who provided the lead vocals on the tour?

1427. Duncan Jones' third film as director, was premiered in Paris, in May 2016, before being released in the US just a month later. Name the film.

1428. At the 'Council of Fashion Designers of America Awards', in June 2016, David was awarded 'The Board Of Directors' Special Tribute Award'. Which actress accepted the award for David?
1429. Following the acceptance speech, who then performed David's iconic track, *Changes?*

1430. On the 10th July 2016, exactly six months after David's passing, a son was born to Duncan and Rodene. What is his name?

1431. At the 'MTV Video Music Awards' at Madison Square Garden, in August 2016, David won 'Best Art Direction' award for the short film/video that accompanied which track from the latest album?

1432. In September 2016, Parlophone released a second box set containing albums, singles, B sides and other edits from David's career, this time from 1974 to 1976. What title was given to the box set?

1433. Exclusive to the box set was the previously unreleased album that eventually became **Young Americans**. Name the album

1434. What was the name of the stage play written and directed by Adrian Berry, and performed by Alex Walton, that opened in London's Waterloo East Theatre in October 2016? It went on to tour the UK for sixteen months.

1435. A soundtrack album from the original cast of 'Lazarus' in New York, was released in October 2016. Which member of the cast received rave reviews for her version of *Life On Mars?*?

1436. First published in November 2016, whose book is entitled 'My Life with Bowie – Spider From Mars'?

the 2010s

1437. Which multinational corporation in London, auctioned off much of David's modern and contemporary art collection, in November 2016? Some reports suggest that they auctioned for a collective £33 million or more.

1438. Which London theatre staged a production of the 'Lazarus' musical between November 2016 and January 2017?

1439. Name the EP that was released posthumously on the Columbia record label, in January 2017, on what would have been David's 70th birthday?

1440. As well as the track *Lazarus,* which had already appeared on the **Blackstar** album, which three other tracks recorded during the same period, also appeared on the EP?

1441. The second of the three BBC documentaries directed by Francis Whately was aired in January 2017. What was its title?

1442. At which awards ceremony held in Los Angeles, in February 2017, did David win four awards, namely 'Best Engineered Album - Non-Classical', 'Best Alternative Music Album', 'Best Rock Song' and 'Best Rock Performance', all for *Blackstar*?

1443. Which designer also won the 'Best Recording Package Award' for his artwork on the album?

ALL MY ~~IDIOT~~ 1500 QUESTIONS

1444. At the 37th 'Brit Awards' ceremony in February 2017, David won the award for 'British Male Solo Artist'. Who presented the award?
1445. Who received the award for David?
1446. Which other award did David win at the same ceremony, for the **Blackstar** album?
1447. Who presented the award?
1448. Who received the award for David?

1449. Marion Skene sadly passed away from cancer in March 2017. In what capacity did Marion fit into the David Bowie story?

1450. In March 2017, the Royal Mail dedicated an entire stamp issue to David. Six of the ten stamps were simply studio album covers. Which six studio album covers were celebrated?
1451. The remaining four stamps depicted David in live concert action. Which four tours did the action shots represent?

1452. Which live double album, recorded at the Universal Amphitheatre Los Angeles, in September 1974, was exclusively issued as part of Record Store Day, in April 2017?

1453. Who directed the documentary film, first released in May 2017, entitled 'Beside Bowie: The Mick Ronson Story'?

1454. As part of BBC Music Day in June 2017, who unveiled the official blue plaque at Hull's Paragon

the 2010s

Station, marking the link between the city and the Spiders from Mars?

1455. The blue plaque was one of three unveiled that day at locations considered pivotal to David's life and career. Who unveiled the blue plaque at the home of the former Trident Studios, in Soho, where both **Hunky Dory** and **The Rise and Fall of Ziggy Stardust and the Spiders from Mars** had been recorded?

1456. In which town was the third plaque unveiled, by The Clash drummer Nick Headon and David's ex-bandmate from the Manish Boys, Bob Solly?

1457. Debuting in August 2017 in his home town of Hull, what was the title of the multimedia show chronicling the life of Mick Ronson? The show was originally conceived as part of the Hull City of Culture 2017 celebrations.

1458. Which track from the **1.Outside** album, was included on the **Spongebob Squarepants** musical soundtrack album, released in September 2017, albeit with altered lyrics?

1459. In September 2017, Parlophone released a third box set containing albums, singles, B sides and other edits from David's career, this time from 1977 to 1982. What title was given to the box set?

1460. Which pianist toured the UK in November 2017, performing all tracks from the **Aladdin Sane** album?
1461. Who made a special guest appearance at four of the six UK shows?

ALL MY ~~IDIOT~~ 1500 QUESTIONS

1462. Which guitarist performed in the band having previously worked with David at 'Live Aid' in 1985, and then again with Tin Machine in 1989?

1463. In recognition of his dad's love for books and literature, what did David's son Duncan announce he was setting up, in December 2017?

1464. What was the name of the 71 episode podcast, created and co-presented by Marc Riley and Rob Hughes, that started broadcasting in January 2018? In their own words, they rifled through the fascinating world of one of the greatest rock stars the world has ever known.

1465. When Elon Musk sent his Tesla Roadstar into space in February 2018, he placed a full sized human mannequin in the driver's seat and called it Starman. The car's sound system was set to continuously loop which of David's songs?

1466. Duncan Jones' final film of the decade was in February 2018 when it was released on Netflix to negative reviews and criticism for its mishandled subject matter. Name the film.

1467. A bronze sculpture (Earthly Messenger) by Andrew Sinclair, was unveiled in March 2018 in the market square of which Buckinghamshire town?

1468. **Welcome To The Blackout** was one of three limited vinyl releases exclusively issued in April 2018, for

the 2010s

Record Store Day. As part of the 'Isolar II' Worldwide Concert Tour, at which London venue and in which year, had the live double album been recorded?

1469. The second vinyl release was a 12" demo of which track from 1983?

1470. The third vinyl release was issued on white vinyl and had the title **Bowie Now**. The album was simply a compilation of 11 tracks taken from which of David's two studio albums released back in the 1970s?

1471. Name the documentary film that was released in 2018, about the small troupe of young, hardcore fans who stood nightly vigil while David was in town during 1974, recording his landmark **Young Americans** album in Philadelphia.

1472. What name did Duncan and Rodene give to David's granddaughter, born to them in April 2018?

1473. Composed in 2018, on which of David's albums did Philip Glass base his **Symphony No. 12**?

1474. Where in July 2018, did the touring 'David Bowie Is' exhibition, finally close its doors?

1475. In October 2018, Parlophone released a fourth box set containing albums, singles, B sides and other edits from David's career, this time from 1983 to 1988. What title was given to the box set?

1476. What was the name of the book, published by photographer Denis O'Regan, in November 2018? It

ALL MY ~~IDIOT~~ 1500 QUESTIONS

comprised a series of photographs taken during the 'Serious Moonlight' Worldwide Concert Tour of 1983.

1477. What was the title of the celebratory show, hosted by long time band member Mike Garson, that took place at Shepherds Bush in January 2019? The show also featured Earl Slick and Gerry Leonard.

1478. Bernard Fowler and Corey Glover shared vocal duties with which Fiction Plane vocalist and bass player?

1479. Gerry Leonard performed a solo version of which **Hunky Dory** track?

1480. In January 2019, in a BBC Two conducted poll, David was the British public's choice for the Greatest Entertainer of the 20th century. Part of the BBC's 'Icons' series, which three other candidates from the world of entertainment shortlist, did David beat?

1481. Which member of one of David's early bands, published a book in January 2019, entitled 'At The Birth Of Bowie'?

1482. The third and final documentary for the BBC trilogy by Francis Whately was broadcast in February 2019. It retraced David's early career in the 1960s through to the fame that came with Ziggy Stardust in the early 1970s. What was the title of the third and final documentary?

1483. In April 2019, which well established streetwear label based in California unveiled a collaborative

the 2010s

collection of footwear and apparel, in tribute to David?

1484. Released in April 2019 on the Parlophone record label, which box set consisted of four 7" vinyls, featuring nine tracks in total, all from 1968?
1485. The name of the box set was taken from a lyric, from which previously unreleased song, which itself featured in the box set?
1486. Complete the titles of these lesser known tracks that also featured in the box set release:-
    a) *Mother* _ _ _ _
    b) *Goodbye* _ _ _ _ _ _ _ _ _ _ _ _ _
    c) *Angel* _ _ _ _ _   _ _ _ _ _ _   _ _ _ _

1487. Record Store Day in April 2019 saw three more vinyl releases. One was a 7" vinyl of *Just A Gigolo* and one was the Decca album, **The World Of David Bowie** on coloured vinyl. What was the third vinyl released that year?

1488. Released in May 2019, on the Parlophone record label, **The Clareville Grove Demos** box set consisted of six tracks, performed back in 1969 at David's Clareville Grove apartment. Who collaborated with David on the recordings?
1489. One of the tracks was *Lover To The Dawn.* Which track had this morphed into by the time of its release on the Philips **David Bowie** album, in 1969?
1490. Of the six tracks, which was the only track not written by David?

ALL MY ~~IDIOT~~ 1500 QUESTIONS

1491. Another Parlophone offering, a box set vinyl album consisting of 10 songs, was released in June 2019. With John 'Hutch' Hutchinson once more the collaborator, what was the title of the box set?
1492. Which song was written by Lesley Duncan?
1493. To what had the track *I'm Not Quite* been re-titled, by the time of its release on the Philips' **David Bowie** album in 1969?

1494. Which famous and popular Mattel toy received a complete make over, in July 2019, replicating the look of David's iconic alter ego, Ziggy Stardust, complete with jumpsuit, red boots and face paint?

1495. A box set entitled **Space Oddity** was released in July 2019 to commemorate the 50th anniversary of the track's original release. Consisting of only two 7" vinyls, the set included original mono versions of *Space Oddity* and *Wild Eyed Boy From Freecloud*, as well as new single edits of the same two tracks, mixed by whom?

1496. In August 2019, to coincide with the 30th anniversary of **Tin Machine**, eight tracks from a June 1989 concert in Paris were released for digital download and streaming. At which famous Paris venue had the concert been recorded?

1497. Published in November 2019, whose book was entitled 'Bowie's Bookshelf – The Hundred Books That Changed David Bowie's Life'?

the 2010s

1498. Parlophone's final box set offering of the decade was a 5-CD box set focusing on David's early development in the late 1960s. Featuring home demos, BBC radio sessions and more (some of which had already been released in box sets earlier in the year), name the box set that was released in November 2019.
1499. One track in the set was called *The Reverend Raymond Brown* followed by what text in brackets?
1500. Complete these lesser known track names, all of which featured on CD1 of the box set:-
    a) *April's* _ _ _ _ _ _ _ _ _ _ _
    b) *Animal* _ _ _ _
    c) *J* _ _ _ _ _ _ _ _
    d) *Hole* _ _ _ _ _ _ _ _ _ _ _

Figure 19: Selection of Picture Discs from Author's Collection, released during the 2010s

Figure 20: Selection of items from Author's Collection, released during the 2010s

the 2010s
200 Answers

1301. Fall Dog Bombs The Moon, Breaking Glass and *China Girl*

1302. David Bowie Deram Album – Deluxe Edition

1303. Absolute Beginners

1304. Live at the Nassau Coliseum

1305. Any Day Now: David Bowie The London Years (1947-1974)

1306. Heroes

1307. Renault Clio (Va Va Voom)

1308. Changes

1309. Source Code

1310. Earl Slick

1311. Mike Garson

1312. Space Oddity

1313. The Legendary Stardust Cowboy

1314. Sarah Ferguson and Raquel Welch

1315. The Jean Genie

1316. Hunky Dory and **Aladdin Sane**

ALL MY ~~IDIOT~~ 1500 QUESTIONS

1317. Gary Kemp
1318. Starman
1319. Speed Of Life
1320. Ken Scott
1321. Jarvis Cocker
1322. Danny Boyle
1323. *Heroes* (a medley of David's songs was also played during the closing ceremony a month later)
1324. Bowiefest
1325. University of Limerick
1326. Rodene Ronquillo
1327. Where Are We Now?
1328. New York artist Tony Oursler
1329. Jacqueline Humphries (Tony Oursler's wife)
1330. M/S Song Of Norway
1331. Floria Sigismondi
1332. Tilda Swinton
1333. The Next Day
1334. Mario J McNulty
1335. "Heroes"
1336. You Feel So Lonely You Could Die
1337. Gail Ann Dorsey
1338. c) Robert Fripp didn't
1339. a) Dancing Out In Space
   b) Love Is Lost
1340. Black Tie White Noise
1341. Boss Of Me
1342. Valentine's Day
1343. Heat
1344. Victoria and Albert Museum, in Cromwell Road, London. (The exhibition is said to have attracted

300,000 visitors in London, and around 2 million visitors worldwide)
1345. Kansai Yamamoto
1346. Victoria Broakes and Geoffrey Marsh
1347. Germany because of his affinity to Berlin
1348. Tim Minchin
1349. *Drive In Saturday*
1350. Chris Hadfield
1351. Five Years
1352. Francis Whately
1353. James Cochran
1354. They were all inducted into the Science Fiction and Fantasy Hall of Fame
1355. Celebrities' faces were donned with the lightning bolt to produce a campaign poster appealing for more blood donors.
1356. *The Next Day*
1357. *Plan*
1358. *Reflektor*
1359. The Reflektors
1360. *Fame*
1361. Nigel Reeve who oversees David's back catalogue
1362. Louis Vuitton
1363. *I'd Rather Be High*
1364. *Where Are We Now?*, *The Stars (Are Out Tonight)*, *The Next Day* and *Valentine's Day*
1365. *Love Is Lost*
1366. British Male Solo Artist (he was 67 years young)
1367. Noel Gallagher
1368. Kate Moss
1369. *Sue (Or In A Season Of Crime)*
1370. *Sunday*

1371. Your Turn To Drive

1372. Shadow Man

1373. 'Tis A Pity She Was A Whore

1374. Robert Peston

1375. O2 Shepherd's Bush Empire

1376. The Man Who Sold The World

1377. Glenn Gregory

1378. Five Years 1969 – 1973

1379. Live Santa Monica '72 and Ziggy Stardust: The Motion Picture

1380. Blackstar

1381. Blackstar

1382. Johan Renck

1383. Elisa Wald-Lasowski

1384. Ziggy Stardust

1385. Lazarus

1386. Enda Walsh

1387. Ivo Van Hove

1388. Michael C. Hall

1389. Lazarus

1390. Steve Lamacq

1391. Celebrity Big Brother

1392. Blackstar

1393. Sue (Or In A Season Of Crime) and 'Tis A Pity She Was A Whore

1394. Dollar Days

1395. Donny McCaslin

1396. Jonathan Barnbrook

1397. Piano

1398. Tim Lefebvre

1399. a) Blackstar
    b) Girl Loves Me

the 2010s

1400. *I Can't Give Everything Away*
1401. Mark Guiliana
1402. *Girl Loves Me*
1403. 10th January 2016
1404. Aynsley Dunbar
1405. Sound And Vision
1406. Starman
1407. *Rebel Rebel*
1408. Rick Wakeman
1409. *Heroes*
1410. *Space Oddity*
1411. Brian Eno
1412. 285 Lafayette Street, Manhattan, New York
1413. *Life On Mars?* and *Space Oddity*
1414. Audi
1415. *The Man Who Sold The World*
1416. *Let's Dance*
1417. Lady Gaga
1418. The Icon Award
1419. Annie Lennox
1420. Gary Oldman
1421. Sterling Campbell, Gail Ann Dorsey, Mike Garson, Gerry Leonard, Catherine Russell and Earl Slick
1422. Lorde
1423. *I Can't Give Everything Away*
1424. Jonathan Barnbrook
1425. Earl Slick
1426. Bernard Fowler
1427. Warcraft
1428. Tilda Swinton
1429. Michael C. Hall
1430. Stenton David Jones

1431. Blackstar
1432. Who Can I Be Now? 1974 – 1976
1433. The Gouster
1434. From Ibiza to the Norfolk Broads
1435. Sophia Anne Caruso
1436. Mick 'Woody' Woodmansey
1437. Sotheby's
1438. King's Cross Theatre
1439. No Plan
1440. No Plan, Killing a Little Time and *When I Met You*
1441. The Last Five Years
1442. 59th Grammy Awards
1443. Jonathan Barnbrook
1444. Zane Lowe
1445. Michael C. Hall
1446. British Album Of The Year
1447. Noel Gallagher
1448. David's son, Duncan
1449. Marion was nanny to Duncan from age 4 onwards
1450. Hunky Dory, Aladdin Sane, "Heroes", Let's Dance, Earthling and Blackstar
1451. 'Ziggy Stardust Tour 1973', 'The Stage Tour 1978','The Serious Moonlight Tour 1983' and 'A Reality Tour 2004'
1452. Cracked Actor
1453. Jon Brewer
1454. Mick 'Woody' Woodmansey
1455. Billy Bragg and George Underwood
1456. Maidstone
1457. Turn And Face The Strange
1458. No Control
1459. A New Career In A New Town 1977 – 1982

1460. Mike Garson
1461. Steve Harley
1462. Kevin Armstrong
1463. An online 'Bowie Book Club'
1464. The A to Z of David Bowie
1465. Space Oddity
1466. Mute
1467. Aylesbury
1468. Earls Court in 1978
1469. *Let's Dance*
1470. Low and "Heroes"
1471. The Sigma Kids
1472. Zowie Tala Mabsie Jones
1473. Lodger
1474. Brooklyn Museum, New York City
1475. Loving The Alien [1983 – 1988]
1476. Ricochet: David Bowie 1983, An Intimate Portrait
1477. A Bowie Celebration – The David Bowie Alumni Tour
1478. Joe Sumner
1479. Andy Warhol
1480. Marilyn Monroe, Charlie Chaplin and Billie Holiday
1481. Phil Lancaster (The Lower Third)
1482. Finding Fame
1483. Vans
1484. Spying Through A Keyhole
1485. Love All Around
1486. a) Mother Grey
    b) Goodbye Threepenny Joe
    c) Angel Angel Grubby Face
1487. **Pin Ups** picture disc
1488. John 'Hutch' Hutchinson
1489. Cygnet Committee

1490. *Life Is A Circus* (Roger Bunn)

1491. The Mercury Demos

1492. Love Song

1493. Letter To Hermione

1494. The Barbie Doll (The David Bowie Barbie Doll)

1495. Tony Visconti

1496. La Cigale

1497. John O'Connell

1498. Conversation Piece

1499. *The Reverend Raymond Brown (Attends the Garden fete on Thatchwick Green)*

1500. a) *April's Tooth Of Gold*
   b) *Animal Farm*
   c) *Jerusalem*
   d) *Hole In The Ground*

AND FINALLY . . .

So there you have it, 1500 questions and answers chronicling the life and times of David Bowie. Did the questions cover everything he's ever done ? Every record he appeared on ? Everyone he ever met ? Of course they didn't, that would be an impossibility, but hopefully there's enough trivia and detail in the book to have given the reader at least some small insight into the life David led, and the extraordinary career he enjoyed.

Obsessive fans may well have known most of the answers, and that's fine, I personally find it reassuring to read about and have confirmed for me, something which I already know. Others may have done better in some decades than in others, and hopefully maybe learned a lot along the way. For any newbie fan coming to David Bowie for the first time, well I envy you, you have a fantastic ~~voyage~~ journey ahead of you and much to look forward to.

Whatever level of fandom you are, I hope you

found the book interesting, informative and both enjoyable and fun to work through. I would like to take a final opportunity to re-iterate once more that the primary purpose of the book has been to raise funds for both the Bowie Bandstand Restoration Appeal in Beckenham, and for Macmillan Cancer Support, so genuine thanks to all who have bought it and contributed to the cause.

AND FINALLY...

David Bowie was a unique talent, the likes of whom we will never see again.

I still miss him.

Printed in Great Britain
by Amazon